Sooner or later we will all make our last journey; some make it knowingly and some have no awareness that they are travelling for the last time. Every day, there are millions of creatures making their final journeys, perhaps seeing the sun or breathing fresh air for the first time, savoring a brief moment of life, before they arrive at their final destination. Travelling should be a pleasure, not a march towards death, as it often is, for the millions of animals transported in trucks and wagons as 'livestock'.

TRAVEL DIFFERENTLY, TRAVEL VEGAN!

A Vegan's Guide to New York City
A 7-day itinerary

by Roberto Rossi

Preface

Getting to know new people is like getting to know new cities. When we first meet someone, we see what is most apparent, most obvious, we can only imagine what lies beneath the surface. Yet we often know intuitively and immediately whether we want to know a new acquaintance better. Cities are the same. The first time we visit a city we can only scratch the surface, we follow the tried and tested tourist routes, we visit the most famous landmarks, only vaguely grasping what makes the place tick, what gives it a soul. With some cities it finishes here. We see the sites, we take the photographs, we go home. With New York one visit is never enough. A lifetime of visits is never enough. There is always more to know, to filter, to unearth.

My favorite people are like New York, with identities that shift when you view them in different lights. One of the first things I knew about Roberto was that he is a photographer, whose pictures offer an unpretentious record of everything that surprises or delights him. Later I discovered that he is also an enthusiastic traveler, who shares my love for the United States. I have crossed the country by train, he has crossed it by car. I spent a happy Italian summer translating his first travel book, Route 66 an America Myth, and discovered that he also has a gift for storytelling. As I got to know him better, more hidden sides came into view. Roberto is a committed animal rights campaigner, a great comedian, a cat owner, a motorcyclist and a vegan whose ethical and environmental convictions are unshakable. When Roberto gives me advice about travelling I listen. He has a gift for knowing exactly what you need to know. My advice to you is to take his advice! Try out the vegan restaurants even if you aren't a strict vegan (like me) and trust him to guide you through New York City.

By Tammy Corkish

Summary

Introduction

New York City is a city of limitless possibility, a mix of cultures and colors, of smells and experiences, an openhearted and chaotic city, a city to love and to hate, a city which refuses to do things by halves.

Fortunately for vegans, New York is extremely welcoming and well organized, offering an array of choice for those who have chosen a vegan lifestyle, whether for health or because of ethical considerations.

For ethical vegans, veganism is much more than a way of eating or following a diet without meat or animal derived products. It goes beyond our choices at lunch or at dinner and represents something much deeper and sincerely felt.

Many of us feel that out of respect for our fellow creatures we should avoid using products obtained from animals completely, including products tested on animals and those that contain hidden animal products.

Luckily, New York City is home to a vast range of vegan friendly eateries, some of which offer vegan options alongside vegetarian dishes or dishes containing meat, and some which are totally vegan.

This guide reflects my love for New York as well as my belief that it is always possible to make choices in keeping with a vegan and eco-friendly lifestyle.

Surprisingly, one of the biggest challenges for the vegan in New York is choosing a hotel that respects our life choices. It is far easier to find a vegan restaurant, bar or cafe offering a moment's rest and nourishment during days spent sightseeing around the city.

This guide is aimed at fellow vegans visiting New York, suggesting daily itineraries for a worry-free vacation full of beautiful new experiences. I offer you my hand to guide you through the streets of the city; we will stop to admire the most famous sites and sample some of the best vegan fare in America.

Guide to the city

New York City doesn't need an introduction, its very name evokes a host of dreams and images. In many ways the symbol of the USA, New York is also unlike any other American metropolis. It is an agglomerate of cultures fused in a vibrant and captivating blend.

Visiting the Big Apple is always an incredible adventure but without planning your trip, you could miss out on the city's most exciting experiences, especially if you are a first-time visitor. So here is a brief guide to the best of New York.

Even if you have never set foot in the city, the names of its streets, sites and buildings will be familiar; Fifth Avenue, Empire State Building, Manhattan Skyline, Time Square, Macy's, Central Park, the Statue of Liberty.

Just close your eyes and images from movies, books and songs about the city will float before you.

New York City is divided into five districts or boroughs: **Manhattan**, the city's beating heart; the **Bronx**, birth place of hip hop and home of the New York Yankees; **Brooklyn**, with its breathtaking views of the Manhattan Skyline from Brooklyn Heights and the beautiful neighborhoods of Williamsburg and DUMBO; **Queens**, founded by the Dutch; and the splendid **Staten Island**.

Manhattan is subdivided into various neighborhoods, some of which are very famous and some of which are less well known but definitely worth a visit.

New York's Districts

New York's most famous neighborhoods are mainly **Downtown**. They are:

- **Wall Street, the Financial District, Lower Manhattan**
- **Seaport & Civic Center, Two Bridges**
- **Chinatown**
- **Little Italy**
- **Lower East Side**
- **Bowery**
- **TriBeCa**
- **SoHo**
- **NoHo**
- **East Village, Alphabet City**
- **NoLIta**
- **Greenwich Village**
- **West Village**
- **Meatpacking District**

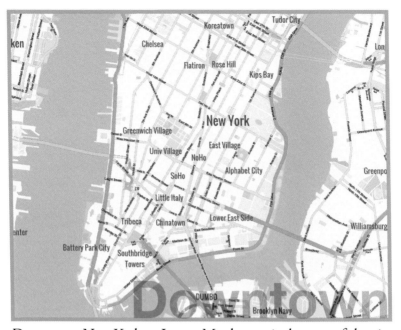

Downtown New York or Lower Manhattan is the part of the city stretching from the point of Manhattan Island on the Hudson River to 14th Street, the area of the original Dutch settlement which was the embryo of the current metropolis. The irregular windings of the streets here seem at odds with the grid layout of the rest of the city and instead of a number, each street has a name. The district's most interesting neighborhoods and sites are: Battery Park, for visiting The Statue of Liberty; chaotic and enchanting Chinatown; Governors Island (which is only open in summer); Greenwich Village; Little Italy; SoHo; Tribeca / Wall Street and The Financial District; The World Trade Center; the Meatpacking District and, between Downtown and Midtown, Roosevelt Island, which you can reach by cable car from East Side.

The most important attractions are the National September 11 Memorial & Museum, Ellis Island, the High Line and the Freedom Tower of the One World Trade Center, Calatrava's Oculus, Brooklyn Bridge and, of course, the Statue of Liberty.

Moving into **Midtown** we find:

- **Chelsea**
- **Gramercy Park, Flatiron District, Kips Bay, Murray Hill**
- **Midtown and Garment District**
- **Hell's Kitchen**

As the name suggests, this is the middle or central part of the city concentrated around Times Square.

Midtown extends from 23rd Street in Chelsea to 59th Street and the south entrance to Central Park. Main attractions include the Empire State Building, Times Square and Grand Central Terminal.

This is New York's main tourist district and is a great place to stay for shopping on Fifth Avenue, visiting MoMa, the Madame Tussauds wax museum, the Chrysler Building, the United Nations Headquarters, Bryant Park, New York Public Library, St Patrick's Cathedral and Top of the Rock and for taking in a show or two on Broadway or at Radio City Music Hall.

Hell's Kitchen, once a den of vice, is now as safe as the rest of New York. Here you can access the High Line, eat in cheaper restaurants and browse the flea market.

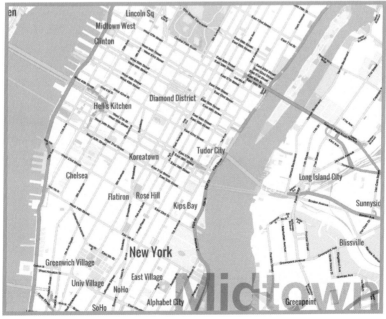

And finally, **Uptown**:
* **Upper East Side**
* **Upper West Side**
* **Harlem**

You could easily spend a week exploring Uptown which includes Central Park; the Metropolitan Museum and the Museum of Natural History; the Dakota Building (on the corner of W 72nd Street and Central Park W); Columbus Circle; the exhilarating neighborhood of Harlem; the Lincoln Center; Morningside Heights and the Guggenheim Museum.

New York's Top 10

If this is your first visit to New York, here are the city's unmissable Top 10 attractions:

1.   **The Statue of Liberty:** by ferry from Battery Park in Lower Manhattan. Many people choose to admire the statue from Battery Park without visiting Liberty Island which if you are strapped for time is a good option. If you want to climb up inside the statue to the crown, you can buy tickets in advance online. Some tickets are sold for immediate entrance, but they are almost impossible to get hold of.

2.   **Ground Zero and the World Trade Center:** the area which was once the site of the Twin Towers is now a tribute to New York's resistance. The memorial is incredible, as is the museum. From the One World Trade Center you can enjoy fantastic views of the city (tickets are available for immediate entrance but it's better to book in advance online). Don't forget to spend some time in the "Oculus" train station, a symbol of the city's rebirth.

3.   **Empire State Building:** even if you probably won't encounter King Kong clinging to the world's most famous skyscraper you will be struck with awe when you see it for the first time. If you don't want to take the elevators to the observatory, spend some time gazing up at the building from the ground. From the observatory there are amazing views, but if you are only going to climb one tower I recommend Top of the Rock.

4.   **Rockefeller Center:** the city within the city. The Rockefeller Center is a complex of 19 buildings (14 of which are original and 5 of which were added in the 1960s and 70s). The most visited attraction is the Top of the Rock experience in the General Electric Building. If you can, visit the observatory at sunset for the best views of Manhattan.

5. **Brooklyn Bridge:** one of New York's icons, Brooklyn Bridge connects Manhattan and Brooklyn. Nothing can compare to the thrill of crossing the bridge for the first time.

6. **Central Park:** the lungs of New York, is a vast green oasis in the center of the city. Take a picnic for a lazy Sunday afternoon or wander for a few hours along the paths and walkways. It is impossible to see the whole park in a day – it covers 3,41 square kilometers. If you want my advice, don't plan! Just enter the park wherever you fancy and get lost in the wilds of New York's biggest green space.

7.   **Times Square:** the belly button of the world! For me this is the center of the planet, the pulsing heart of Manhattan, a riot of billboards and neon signs, crazy crowds and the ideal place to start your visit. Leave your bags at the hotel and head straight here, nothing is more New York than Times Square.

8.   **High Line and the Meatpacking District:** the hippest neighborhood in New York. It is hard to believe that only a few years ago this area was rundown and almost deserted. It is now one of the trendiest places on Earth. Take a walk along the High Line and see the city from a whole new angle.

9.   **SoHo and the Village:** for me, these are New York's most beautiful neighborhoods, places where you can lose yourself gazing at the cast iron buildings, visiting the art galleries and watching the street artists. Nothing could seem further than the chaotic roar of the city.

10.   **Wall Street:** the financial district and international banking center. Take a walk to Federal Hall where George Washington was sworn in as the USA's first president.

It's impossible to get bored in New York. However much time you spend here it's never enough. Most people stay for a maximum of five to seven days which will fly by. To make the most of your trip it's really important to organize your time.

New York's Subway is easy and cheap to use. If you are staying for a few days, buy a travelcard for unlimited travel.

You could spend an entire day in many of New York's museums which are perfect for rainy weather and often have free entrance times. MoMa, for example, is free on Fridays from 16:00 to 21:00.

If you are visiting Wall Street, try to go on a weekday as the offices are all closed at the weekend and the atmosphere is hardly the same with only the odd tourist milling about; Broadway and Times Square are particularly busy before shows start and when they finish. Wednesday is matinee day on Broadway.

On the day you arrive, I advise you to explore the area around your hotel. Get over your travel weariness and jetlag before venturing further afield. If you are arriving from a European time zone, try and adjust by going to bed as late possible. The first day you will probably wake up at 5 in the morning, but your biological clock will quickly reset itself.

New York is best seen from its streets so try and walk as much as you can. Only use the subway for longer trips. Take a good pair of walking shoes or sneakers and don't be afraid of wearing them out.

In New York streets go from East to West and Avenues go from North to South. Apart from Lower Manhattan, every street and every avenue have a number which makes navigating the city very easy.

Practical tips

First of all, when you are in New York and in the USA in general, always leave a tip! In American culture tipping isn't optional, it's expected. In restaurants and bars with table service you should always tip your waiter or waitress. In your hotel you should tip the porter and anyone else who provides you with a personal service. The only exception is in fast food restaurants or when you buy food from street vendors.

When you eat in a restaurant you should add 10% to 20% to the bill; in your hotel, you should leave a few dollars for room service when you leave and give the porter a dollar for each bag he carries.

If you bring European electrical appliances to the **USA**, you will need an adaptor to fit the US electrical receptacles. You may also need a converter to change the voltage from 110 volts to 220 volts. Most common appliances will function with either 50 or 60 cycle current.

You should be able to use your **cell phone in the USA**, check with your operator before you leave. For internet there are many free hotspots or you could consider buying an American SIM card (I recommend H2O).

The prefix for calling the USA is +1. If you call Europe, remember the time difference!

Health Insurance
Don't risk travelling without it! The American health system is very modern and efficient but unlike European health services, it isn't free. If you need medical care while you are in the USA and you don't have insurance, you will have to pay for it.

Passports, Visas and ESTA
Before you leave your own country, you must receive authorization for travelling to the USA. Most European citizens can use ESTA

(the Electronic System for Travel Authorization). You can submit an authorization request on the ESTA website. The service costs 14 dollars and, once granted, authorization lasts for two years. At present the citizens of 38 countries are eligible for ESTA. Citizens of other countries need a visa to enter the USA.

Besides ESTA, visitors to the USA must have an electronic passport and a return ticket dated no more than 90 days after their date of arrival.

All visitors are required to give their fingerprints and have their photograph taken when they arrive.

In some airports, including JFK, there are automatic terminals for travelers in possession of ESTA who have already visited the USA. If you can, it is worth using these terminals, which will issue you with a receipt for customs, as you can avoid the queues and collect your bags more quickly.

Travelling from the airport

New York's airports are well connected to the city center. Most international visitors arrive at JFK, from where you can take a taxi, a shuttle or public transport to your hotel. I prefer using public transport which is usually faster and cheaper than a taxi or a private or shared shuttle.

Taxi rides to the center have a fixed price of 52 dollars which doesn't include toll charges or tips.

Shared shuttle rides to hotels in the city cost around 20/25 dollars.

Public transport is your best option if you don't have too much luggage; from JFK take the AirTrain to Jamaica or Howard Beach and take the subway to the station nearest to your hotel.

From Jamaica / Sutphin Boulevard line E will take you into Manhattan via most of the most popular tourist stops; while from Howard Beach, Line A will take you to Manhattan.

When to visit New York
Always, in every season, as soon as you can. If you go in the summer, prepare for the heat, while in winter remember that the temperature can dip below zero and cold Atlantic winds blow through the city's streets.
My favorite seasons in New York are spring and fall which have mild temperatures and days long enough to enjoy being outside.

Where to eat
New York has a restaurant for every taste; it doesn't matter whether you are looking for fine dining, avantgarde experimental cooking, ethnic cuisine, traditional fast food, healthy or organic dishes or street fare, you will be spoilt for choice.
Nearly all restaurants display a sign indicating their rating by the New York City Department of Health and Mental Hygiene. Restaurants fall into three categories, A, B and C with A representing the highest standards of food preparation and hygiene and C the lowest acceptable level.
You are safe with A and B but might want to avoid C. A 'Grade Pending' sign means that the restaurant has made a request for a B or C grading to be reconsidered and is awaiting a legal decision.
Fortunately for vegans there is a huge choice in New York. Below is a list of New York's vegan friendly restaurants. For ease of reference, I've divided them into three categories: 100 % Vegan, Vegetarian with Vegan Options and Restaurants which serve Vegan Dishes. The list was last updated in July 2018.

Pizzeria Restaurant Fast Food Caffè Market

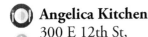 **Angelica Kitchen**
300 E 12th St,
New York 10003
tel: +1 212-228-2909
web: www.angelicakitchen.com

Arata 67
2nd Ave, New York,
NY 10003
tel: +1 212-698-1948
web: www.matthewkenneycuisine.com

Avant Garden
East Village 130 E 7th St,
New York 10009
tel: +1 646-922-7948
web: www.avantgardennyc.com

Avant Garden Williamsburg
188 Havemeyer St,
Brooklyn 11211
tel: +1 929-276-3002
web: www.avantgardennyc.com

Bar Verde
65 2nd Ave,
New York, NY 10003
tel: +1 212-777-6965
web: www.barverdenyc.com

Beyond Sushi
70 Pine St,
New York 10005
tel: +1 917-261-4530
web: www.beyondsushinyc.com

Beyond Sushi
229 E 14th St,
New York 10003
tel: +1 646-861-2889
web: www.beyondsushinyc.com

Beyond Sushi
62 W 56th St,
New York 10019
tel: +1 646-964-5097
web: www.beyondsushinyc.com

Beyond Sushi
134 W 37th St,
New York 10018
tel: +1 212-564-0869
web: www.beyondsushinyc.com

Beyond Sushi
Chelsea Market, 75 9th
Ave New York 10011
tel: +1 212-929-2889
web: www.beyondsushinyc.com

Blossom
187 9th Ave,
New York 10011
tel: +1 212-627-1144
web: www.blossomnyc.com

Blossom Du Jour
617 9th Ave,
New York 10036
tel: +1 646-998-3535

Blossom Du Jour
259 W 23rd St,
New York 10011
tel: +1 212-229-2595
web: www.blossomdujour.com

Blossom Du Jour Express
1000 8th Ave,
New York 10019
tel: +1 212-765-6500
web: www.blossomdujour.com

Blossom Du Jour
449 Amsterdam Ave,
New York 10024
tel: +1 212-712-9822
web: www.blossomdujour.com

Blossom on Columbus
507 Columbus Ave,
New York 10024
tel: +1 212-875-2600
web: www.blossomnyc.com

Bodhi
77 Mulberry St,
New York 10013
tel: +1 212-233-2921
web: www.buddhavegetarian.com

by CHLOE.
22nd Street 60 W 22nd St,
New York 10010
tel: +1 347-620-9622
web: www.eatbychloe.com

by CHLOE. SoHo
240 Lafayette St,
New York 10012
tel: +1 347-620-9620
web: www.eatbychloe.com

by CHLOE. Williamsburg
171 N 3rd St,
Brooklyn 11211
tel: +1 347-379-4828
web: www.eatbychloe.com

Sweets by CHLOE.
185 Bleecker St B,
New York 10012
tel: +1 347-620-9621
web: www.eatbychloe.com

**by CHLOE.
Rockefeller Center**
1 Rockefeller Plaza,
New York 10020
tel: +1 646-453-7181
web: www.eatbychloe.com

Candle 79
154 E 79th St,
New York 10075
tel: +1 212-537-7179
web: www.candle79.com

Caravan Of Dreams
405 E 6th St,
New York 10009
tel: +1 212-254-1613
web: www.caravanofdreamsnyc.com

Champs Diner
197 Meserole St, Brooklyn 11206
tel: +1 718-599-2743
web: www.champsdiner.com

Cienfuegos
95 Avenue A,
New York, NY 10009
tel: +1 212-614-6818
web: www.cienfuegosny.com/home

Double Zero
65 2nd Ave,
New York 10003
tel: +1 212-777-1608
web: www.matthewkenneycuisine.com

Dun-Well Doughnuts
222 Montrose Ave,
Brooklyn 11206
tel: +1 347-294-0871
web: www.dunwelldoughnuts.com

Dun-Well Doughnuts
102 St Marks Pl,
New York 10009
tel: +1 646-998-5492
web: www.dunwelldoughnuts.com

Erin McKenna's Bakery
NYC 248 Broome St,
New York 10002
tel: +1 855-462-2292
web: www.erinmckennasbakery.com

Franchia Vegan Cafe
12 Park Ave,
New York 10016
tel: +1 212-213-1001
web: www.franchia.com

Jivamukte Cafe
841 Broadway East Side,
New York 10003
(yoga e ristorante Vegan)
tel: +1 212-353-0214
web: www.jivamukteacafe.com

Little Choc Apothecary
141 Havemeyer St,
Brooklyn 11211
tel: +1 718-963-0420
web: www.littlechoc.nyc

Marty's V Burger Restaurant
134 E 27th St,
New York 10016
tel: +1 646-484-6325
web: www.martysvburger.com

Mother of Pearl
95 Avenue A,
New York, NY 10009,
tel: +1 212-614-6818
web:www.motherofpearlnyc.com

Modern Love
317 Union Ave,
Brooklyn 11211
tel: +1 929-298-0626
web: www.modernlovebrooklyn.com

Peacefood Cafe
460 Amsterdam Ave,
New York 10024
tel: +1 212-362-2266
web: www.peacefoodcafe.com

Peacefood
41 E 11th St,
New York 10003
tel: +1 212-979-2288
web: www.peacefoodcafe.com

PLANTMADE
152 2nd Ave,
New York, NY 10003
tel: +1 646-461-2124
web: www.matthewkenneycuisine.com

Sacred Crow
227 Sullivan St,
New York 10012
tel: +1 212-337-0863
web: www.sacredchow.com

Screamer's Pizzeria
620 Manhattan Ave,
Brooklyn 11222
tel: +1 347-844-9412
web: www.screamerspizzeria.com

Seasoned Vegan
55 St Nicholas Ave,
New York 10026
tel: +1 212-222-0092
web: www.seasonedvegan.com

Terri
60 W 23rd St,
New York 10010
tel: +1 212-647-8810
web: www.terrinyc.com

Terri
685 3rd Ave,
New York 10017
tel: +1 212-983-2200

Terri
100 Maiden Ln,
New York 10038
tel: +1 212-742-7901
web: www.terrinyc.com

The Cinnamon Snail
7th Ave & West 33rd Street,
New York 10005
web: www.cinnamonsnail.com

The Cinnamon Snail in City Acres Market
70 Pine Street,
New York 10270
tel: +1 917-261-4530
web: www.cinnamonsnail.com

The Cinnamon Snail
2 Pennsylvania Plaza,
New York, NY 10121
tel: +1 917-261-4530
web: www.cinnamonsnail.com

Vegetarian with Vegan Options:

The Organic Grill
123 1st Avenue,
New York 10003
tel: +1 212-477-7177
web: www.theorganicgrill.com

Uptown Veg
52 E 125th St,
New York, NY 10035
tel: +1 212-987-2660
web: www.facebook.com/Uptown-
Veg-374509442644237

Urban | Vegan Kitchen
41 Carmine St,
New York 10014
tel: +1 646-438-9939
web: www.urbanvegankitchen.com

XYST
44 W 17th St,
New York, NY 10011
tel: +1 212-727-2979
web: www.matthewkenneycuisine.com

Buddha Bodai
5 Mott St,
New York 10013
tel: +1 212-566-8388
web: www.bodai.com

Cocoa V Chocolate
174 9th Ave,
New York 10011
tel: +1 646-998-3130

Dirt Candy
86 Allen St,
New York 10002
tel: +1 212-228-7732
web: www.dirtcandynyc.com

Hangawi
12 E 32nd St,
New York 10016
tel: +1 212-213-0077
web: www.hangawirestaurant.com

Ladybird
111 E 7th St,
New York 10009
tel: +1 917-261-5524
web: www.ladybirdny.com

Maoz
38 Union Square E,
New York 10003
tel: +1 212-260-1988
web: www.maozusa.com

Maoz

683 8th Ave,
New York 10036
tel: +1 212-265-2315
web: www.maozusa.com

Maoz Falafel & Grill
558 7th Ave,
New York 10018
tel: +1 212-777-0820
web: www.maozusa.com

Maoz Vegetarian
5th Ave & E 106th St,
New York 10029
web: www.maozusa.com

Nix
72 University Pl,
New York 10003
tel: +1 212-498-9393
web: www.nixny.com

Orchard Grocer
78 Orchard St,
New York 10002
tel: +1 646-757-9910
web: www.orchardgrocer.com

Superiority Burger
430 E 9th St,
New York 10009
tel: +1 212-256-1192
web: www.superiorityburger.com

Taim West Village
22 Waverly Pl,
New York 10014
tel: +1 212-691-1287
web: www.taimfalafel.com

Taïm Nolita
45, 4106, 4106, Spring St,
New York 10012
tel: +1 212-219-0600
web: www.taimfalafel.com

The Butcher's Daughter
19 Kenmare St,
New York 10012
tel: +1 212-219-3434
web: www.thebutchersdaughter.com

The Butcher's Daughter
581 Hudson St,
New York 10014
tel: +1 917-388-2132
web: www.thebutchersdaughter.com

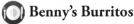 **Restaurants which serve Vegan Dishes:**

Benny's Burritos
113 Greenwich Ave,
New York 10014
tel: +1 212-633-9210
web: www.blockheads.com

Blockheads
60 3rd Ave,
New York 10003
tel: +1 917-388-3534
web: www.blockheads.com

Blockheads Burritos
954 2nd Ave,
New York 10022
tel: +1 212-750-2020
web: www.blockheads.com

Blockheads
1563 2nd Ave,
New York 10028
tel: +1 212-879-1999
web: www.blockheads.com

Blockheads
322 W 50th St,
New York 10019
tel: +1 212-307-7029
web: www.blockheads.com

Blockheads
175 W 90th St,
New York 10024
tel: +1 212-510-7410
web: www.blockheads.com

Brooklyn Bagel & Coffee Company
286 8th Ave,
New York 10001
tel: +1 212-924-2824
web: www.bkbagel.com

Brooklyn Bagel & Coffee Company
35-09 Ditmars Blvd,
Long Island City 11105
tel: +1 718-932-8280
web: www.bkbagel.com

Brooklyn Bagel & Coffee Company
3505 Broadway,
Astoria 11106
tel: +1 718-204-0141
web: www.bkbagel.com

Brooklyn Grange
63 Flushing Ave,
Brooklyn, NY 11205
tel: +1 347-670-3660
web: www.brooklyngrangefarm.com

Brooklyn Grange
37-18 Northern Blvd,
Long Island City, NY 11101
tel: +1 347-670-3660
web: www.brooklyngrangefarm.com

Chalk Point Kitchen
527 Broome St,
New York 10013
tel: +1 212-390-0327
web: www.chalkpointkitchen.com

Dumpling Man
100 St Marks Pl,
New York 10009
tel: +1 212-505-2121
web: www.dumplingman.com

Ess-a-Bagel
831 3rd Ave,
New York 10022
tel: +1 212-980-1010
web: www.a-bagel.com

fresh&co
1260 Lexington Ave,
New York 10028
tel: +1 212-953-7374
web:www.freshandco.com

fresh&co
475 Lexington Ave,
New York 10017
tel: +1 212-867-2333
web:www.freshandco.com

fresh&co
200 W 57th St,
New York 10019
tel: +1 212-513-7374
web:www.freshandco.com

fresh&co
127 E 60th St,
New York 10022
tel: +1 212-663-7374
web:www.freshandco.com

fresh&co
8701, 1211 6th Ave,
New York 10036
tel: +1 212-768-8080
web:www.freshandco.com

fresh&co
425 Park Ave S,
New York 10016
tel: +1 212-233-7374
web:www.freshandco.com

fresh&co
309 Madison Ave,
New York 10017
tel: +1 212-533-7374
web:www.freshandco.com

fresh&co
363 7th Ave,
New York 10001
tel: +1 212-333-7374
web:www.freshandco.com

fresh&co
1359 Broadway,
New York 10018
tel: +1 212-253-7374
web:www.freshandco.com

fresh&co
569 Lexington Ave,
New York 10022
tel: +1 212-223-2670
web:www.freshandco.com

fresh&co
729 Broadway,
New York 10003
tel: +1 212-473-7374
web:www.freshandco.com

Hotel Tortuga
246 E 14th St,
New York 10003
tel: +1 212-228-1884
web: www.hoteltortuganyc.com

John's of 12th Street
302 E 12th St,
New York 10003
tel: +1 212-475-9531
web: www.johnsof12thstreet.com

Juliana's
19 Old Fulton St,
Brooklyn, NY 11201
tel: +1 718-596-6700
web: www.julianaspizza.com

Kesté Pizza & Vino
271 Bleecker St,
New York, NY 10014
tel: +1 212-243-1500
web: www.kestepizzeria.com

Kesté Pizza & Vino
66 Gold St.
New York, NY 10038
tel: +1 212-693-9030
web: www.kestepizzeria.com

Mamoun's
30 St Marks Pl,
New York 10003
tel: +1 646-870-5785
web: www.mamouns.com

Mamoun's
119 Macdougal St,
New York 10012
web: www.mamouns.com

Mamoun's Falafel
300 Washington St,
Hoboken, NJ 07030
tel: +1 201-656-0310
web: www.mamouns.com

Peas & Pickles
55 Washington St,
Brooklyn, NY 11201
tel: +1 718-488-8336
web: www.dumbo.is

S'MAC
East Village 197 1st Avenue,
New York 10003
tel: +1 212-358-7912
web: www.smacnyc.com

Sweetgreen
50 Washington St,
Brooklyn, NY 11201
tel: +1 347-757-4900
web: www.sweetgreen.com

Sweetgreen
67 Wall St,
New York, NY 10005
tel: +1 212-487-9030
web: www.sweetgreen.com

Sweetgreen
100 Kenmare St,
New York, NY 10012
tel: +1 646-964-5012
web: www.sweetgreen.com

Sweetgreen
226 Bleecker St,
New York, NY 10014
tel: +1 917-639-3212
web: www.sweetgreen.com

Sweetgreen
101 University Pl,
New York, NY 10003
tel: +1 917-832-1900
web: www.sweetgreen.com

Sweetgreen
10 Astor Pl,
New York, NY 10003
tel: +1 646-692-3112
web: www.sweetgreen.com

Sweetgreen
413 Greenwich St,
New York, NY 10013
tel: +1 646-922-8572
web: www.sweetgreen.com

Sweetgreen
1164 Broadway,
New York, NY 10001
tel: +1 646-449-8884
web: www.sweetgreen.com

Sweetgreen
162 N 4th St,
Brooklyn, NY 11211
tel: +1 347-987-3863
web: www.sweetgreen.com

Sweetgreen
8 E 18th St,
New York, NY 10003
tel: +1 646-692-3131
web: www.sweetgreen.com

Sweetgreen
32 Gansevoort St,
New York, NY 10014
tel: +1 646-891-5100
web: www.sweetgreen.com

Sweetgreen
66 E 55th St,
New York, NY 10022
tel: +1 646-859-0100
web: www.sweetgreen.com

Sweetgreen
1384 Broadway,
New York, NY 10021
tel: +1 212-334-3020
web: www.sweetgreen.com

Sweetgreen
137 E 61st St,
New York, NY 10065
tel: +1 646-859-1300
web: www.sweetgreen.com

Sweetgreen
311 Amsterdam Ave,
New York, NY 10023
tel: +1 212-496-4081
web: www.sweetgreen.com

Sweetgreen
1321 1st Avenue,
New York, NY 10021
tel: +1 646-585-0900
web: www.sweetgreen.com

Sweetgreen
1500 3rd Ave,
New York, NY 10028
tel: +1 646-666-0860
web: www.sweetgreen.com

Sweetgreen
1114 6th Ave,
New York, NY 10036
tel: +1 917-993-5070
web: www.sweetgreen.com

Sweetgreen
2937 Broadway,
New York, NY 10025
tel: +1 917-675-6616
web: www.sweetgreen.com

Sweetgreen
2460 Broadway,
New York, NY 10025
tel: +1 917-934-3200
web: www.sweetgreen.com

Two Boots Hell's Kitchen
625 9th Ave,
New York 10036
tel: +1 212-956-2668
web: www.twoboots.com

Two Boots
42 Avenue A,
New York 10009
tel: +1 212-254-1919
web: www.twoboots.com

Two Boots
337 Lexington Ave,
New York 10016
tel: +1 212-557-7992
web: www.twoboots.com

Two Boots
201 W 11th St,
New York 10014
tel: +1 212-633-9096
web: www.twoboots.com

Two Boots
Upper East Side
1617 2nd Ave,
New York 10028
tel: +1 212-734-0317
web: www.twoboots.com

Two Boots
2547 Broadway,
New York 10025
tel: +1 212-280-2668
web: www.twoboots.com

Two Boots Pizza
133 Newark Ave,
Jersey City, NJ 07302
tel: +1 201-209-1250
web: www.twoboots.com

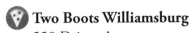

Two Boots Williamsburg
558 Driggs Ave,
Brooklyn 11211
tel: +1 718-387-2668
web: www.twoboots.com

Two Boots
284 5th Ave,
Brooklyn 11215
tel: +1 718-499-0008
web: www.twoboots.com

Urbanspace
at 570 Lex General Electric
Building
570 Lexington Ave,
New York 10022
tel: +1 917-388-9564
web: www.urbanspacenyc.com

Vanessa's Dumpling House
118 Eldridge St,
New York 10002
tel: +1 212-625-8008
web: www.vanessas.com

Vanessa's Dumpling House
220 E 14th St,
New York 10003
tel: +1 212-529-1329
web: www.vanessas.com

Vanessa's Dumpling House
310 Bedford Ave,
Brooklyn 11211
tel: +1 718-218-8809
web: www.vanessas.com

Whole Foods Market
10 Columbus Circle
Ste Sc101,
New York 10019
tel: +1 212-823-9600
web: www.wholefoodsmarket.com

Whole Foods Market
100 W 125th St,
New York 10027
tel: +1 212-678-1940
web: www.wholefoodsmarket.com

Whole Foods Market
808 Columbus Ave,
New York 10025
tel: +1 212-222-6160
web: www.wholefoodsmarket.com

Whole Foods Market
1551 3rd Ave,
New York 10128
tel: +1 646-891-3888
web: www.wholefoodsmarket.com

Whole Foods Market
226 E 57th St,
New York 10022
tel: +1 646-497-1222
web: www.wholefoodsmarket.com

Whole Foods Market
270 Greenwich St,
New York 10007
tel: +1 212-349-6555
web: www.wholefoodsmarket.com

Whole Foods Market
905 River Rd,
Edgewater, NJ 07020
tel: +1 201-941-4000
web: www.wholefoodsmarket.com

Whole Foods Market
1095 6th Ave,
New York 10036
tel: +1 917-728-5700
web: www.wholefoodsmarket.com

Whole Foods Market
250 7th Ave,
New York 10001
tel: +1 212-924-5969
web: www.wholefoodsmarket.com

Whole Foods Market
Zeckendorf Towers
4 Union Square E,
New York 10003
tel: +1 212-673-5388
web: www.wholefoodsmarket.com

Whole Foods Market
95 E Houston St,
New York 10002
tel: +1 212-420-1320
web: www.wholefoodsmarket.com

Whole Foods Market
238 Bedford Ave,
Brooklyn 11249
tel: +1 718-734-2321
web: www.wholefoodsmarket.com

Arata

67 2nd Ave,
New York, NY 10003
tel: +1 212-698-1948
www.matthewkenneycuisine.com

Arata's menu includes steamed buns, small plates, noodle bowls, tempura and beautiful desserts. They also serve cocktails and sake. The restaurant only uses plant-based ingredients from Asian and especially Japanese culinary traditions.

Bar Verde

65 2nd Ave,
New York, NY 10003
tel: +1 212-777-6965
www.barverdenyc.com

In the heart of East Village, Matthew Kenney's Bar Verde blends the chef's passion for vegan cooking with Latin American and particularly Mexican food. Enjoy the array of sharing plates which include guacamoles, ceviche, chips and dips, a complete taco menu and a wide choice of main dishes. The restaurant also serves organic cocktails tequila and mezcal. The atmosphere is relaxed and casual.

Brooklyn Grange

63 Flushing Ave,
Brooklyn, NY 11205
tel: +1 347-670-3660
www.brooklyngrangefarm.com

Brooklyn Grange, a leader in the field of urban green design, manages rooftop gardens and farms in New York City producing more than 22.000 kg of organic food a year.

As well as cultivating and distributing their products, the company organizes educational events, offers consultancy services and collaborates with many no-profit organizations in the city and beyond.

Visit the Brooklyn Grange website for information about where to buy their products, where to find restaurants that use their fruits and vegetables and how to take part in events. Farm dinners sell out very quickly so book as soon as you can.

The Cinnamon Snail

100% Vegan

Various locations, see the restaurant list for details
web: www.cinnamonsnail.com

Cinnamon Snail came into being in 2010 as America's first vegan organic food truck. It is now one of the most well-known vegan pitstops in New York. The company has two mobile trucks, a restaurant in The Pennsy food hall on 33rd / 7th, and a location in FiDi inside City Acres Market on the corner of Cedar & Pearl.

They are 100%, vegan only use the best quality products and tell stories of broccoli kings and queens who live in carrot castles on their website.

Cinnamon Snail has won numerous awards and has received accolades from the New York Times, the Food Network and other publications and TV channels. We strongly recommend their donuts.

Double Zero
100% Vegan

65 2nd Ave,
New York 10003
tel: +1 212-777-1608
www.matthewkenneycuisine.com

Double Zero makes the world's favorite food a healthy choice, serving pizzas cooked in a purpose-built wood-burning oven.

Located in East Village, this veggie-centered Italian restaurant, also serves vegan cheeses made from nuts as well as herb-based desserts and organic wines from Europe produced using sustainable farming methods. The atmosphere is warm and informal. Coming soon are branches in Boston, Philadelphia, Brooklyn and Los Angeles.

Franchia Vegan Cafe
100% Vegan

12 Park Ave,
New York 10016
tel: +1 212-213-1001
www.franchia.com

Franchia only uses vegetable products in preparing its innovative Asian (mainly Korean) inspired dishes. All its dishes are vegan.

The cafe is a multi-level space which offers a beautiful and uniquely Zen dining experience. For tea lovers there is a huge selection of green, black and oolong blends as well as herbal infusions.

John's of 12th Street

$ 302 E 12th St,
$ New York 10003
tel: +1 212-475-9531
www.johnsof12thstreet.com

Little Choc Apothecary

100% Vegan

$ 141 Havemeyer St,
$ Brooklyn 11211
tel: +1 718-963-0420
www.littlechoc.nyc

Founded in 1908, this restaurant has a long tradition of serving genuine Italian food, including vegetarian and vegan sauces. Originally a small room with a kitchen run by an Italian immigrant, Giovanni, and his wife (Momma John), the restaurant fronted an upstairs speakeasy during Prohibition. The entire second floor was reserved for customers who ordered 'dessert'. You can still see the door, now sealed off, which led to the speakeasy upstairs where Momma John served beer and spirits. This enterprising woman used to make liquor in a small shed on the premises and wine in the basement. A system of pulleys was used to hoist the alcoholic drinks to the second floor without spilling a drop in the restaurant which always passed as perfectly above board.

Little Choc Apothecary is NYC's first fully vegan and gluten free creperie. It has a wide range of savory and sweet crepes as well as homemade baked goods. Everything it sells is 100% plant based without chemical binders, gums, artificial flavors and overly processed sugars and flours. The company sources its ingredients from farms and distributors committed to sustainability and when possible uses local, organic and fair-trade products. They also serve biodynamic wines and beers, fresh juices, Toby's Estate coffee and tea blends for health and wellbeing. They have over 100 herb varieties so that guests can request off menu tea blends to suit their own needs and tastes. They also sell tea by the ounce for brewing at home.

Nix

72 University Pl,
New York 10003
tel: +1 212-498-9393
www.nixny.com

Nix is a prize winning vegetarian and vegan restaurant in Greenwich Village with a Michelin star. Head chef is John Fraser, whose philosophy is that cooking without meat is a gain not a loss.

The creative cocktail list, the excellent service and the stress-free ambience make dining here a fantastic experience.

Orchard Grocer

78 Orchard St,
New York 10002
tel: +1 646-757-9910
www.orchardgrocer.com

Orchard Grocer is a 100% vegan and palm oil free deli, which sells products difficult to find elsewhere. Its amazing sandwich selection includes The Bowery with turmeric tofu, tempeh bacon and Violife provolone and The Monty with hunter gatherer mortadella, Violife provolone, roasted peppers, olives, lettuce, tomato and mayo. Also try the desserts by Om Sweet Om.

Terri

100% Vegan

$ Various locations, see the restaurant list for details
www.terrinyc.com

Terri is the first of its kind. The company's founders both have mom's named Terri who instilled in them the importance of wholesome food. Now they are bringing mom's cooking to people on the go. They serve great sandwiches, fresh juices and delicious desserts. They have three locations: Chelsea (60 West 23rd Street), the Financial District (100 Maiden Lane) and Midtown East (685 3rd Ave). All items are 100% vegan.

Two Boots

$ Various locations, see the restaurant list for details
www.twoboots.com

Two Boots was founded in East Village in 1987 by two Indie filmmakers who love pizza, beer and everything about New Orleans. Its name refers to the geographical shapes of Italy and Louisiana. The company now has restaurants in New York, New Jersey, Los Angeles and Nashville which serve a mix or Cajun-Italian cooking. All their restaurants have a family friendly atmosphere and a funky art feel.

Two Boots has been a pioneer in vegan pizzas since the 1980s. One of its founders, Doris Kornish, is a lifelong vegetarian and its menu includes many meat and cheese free options as well as many unusual vegetables. Over the years the range of vegan pizzas and pies has grown to become a whole sub section of the menu. You can choose from 6 standard vegan pizzas. For a special treat go for the V for Vegan pizza.

Marty's V Burger Restaurant

100% Vegan

134 E 27th St,
New York 10016
tel: +1 646-484-6325
web: www.martysvburger.com

Marty's V Burger is a vegan Fast Food concept based in New York City. They are proud to serve vegan, cruelty-free versions of classic comfort food like burgers, fries, mac and cheese, and "chicken" drumstix. Their flagship restaurant has been open since July 2017 on East 27th st. in Midtown Manhattan.

XYST

100% Vegan

44 W 17th St,
New York, NY 10011
tel: +1 212-727-2979
www.matthewkenneycuisine.com

XYST offers a menu inspired by Mediterranean cooking and cocktails from the Matthew Kenney Cuisine team.

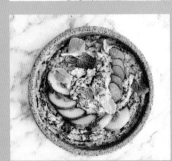

Where to sleep

New York has one of the highest concentrations of hotels in the world, yet, despite extensive research, I have only found two which I would describe as totally vegan friendly.
I contacted hundreds of hotels, all of which replied. Many were understanding of my life choices and offered a selection of vegan dining options but hardly any could guarantee that they used no animal products in the hotel. This was especially the case for furnishings and cleaning products.

Let's begin with the star of New York's ecologically aware hotels, the only one which can boast an interior completely devoid of animal products, which runs 100% on renewable energy and which recycles its waste.

Element New York Times Square West
311 W 39th Street 10018 NY
http://www.elementhotels.com

This is not actually a vegan hotel in that the restaurant offers non-vegan dishes as well as vegan options. What is commendable about Element New York Times Square West is its commitment to the environment. The entire hotel is designed with sustainability and the environment in mind, without compromising service or comfort.

All the kitchens are certified ENERGY STAR®, the bathrooms are designed to minimize waste and there are containers for collecting and recycling trash. The hotel's water filter system reduces the need to serve bottled water, the restaurant uses traditional plates and cutlery instead of paper and plastic and the showers have shampoo and shower gel dispensers instead of single use sachets.

The hotel's large windows and open spaces let in as much natural light as possible, and its energy saving lightbulbs emit a low and relaxing light, using 75% less energy than traditional lighting. The hotel only uses environmentally friendly cleaning products. The building is LEED (Leadership in Energy and Environmental Design) certified.

Hotel Beacon is also completely furnished in synthetic materials.

It doesn't offer breakfast, but each room has a small kitchenette.

Hotel Beacon NYC
2130 Broadway at 75th Street 10023 NY
http://www.beaconhotel.com

The hotel is on the Upper West Side of Manhattan, in a neighborhood of tree-lined avenues filled with excellent restaurants and sidewalk cafes. It is ideally placed for shopping at "The Shops at Columbus Circle".

The Beacon is within walking distance of the Lincoln Center, Central Park, the American Museum of Natural History and the Rose Center for Earth and Space and is one subway stop away from Times Square.

The Beacon has a warm and contemporary feel, with 278 rooms and suites, each with a kitchenette. The suites all have sofa beds making them ideal for families. Fairway Market across the street is good for quick meals and snacks.

Coffee and tea are provided, and all rooms have a safe, a flat screen 32" HD TV, heating and air conditioning, soundproof windows, complimentary Gilchrist & Soames toiletries, irons and hairdryers.

The Viand Café restaurant in the hotel serves meals and the Beacon Bar also serves food. The hotel has a fitness center and laundry service as well as free Wi-fi.

And that's it! Apart from these two hotels, I didn't manage to find any that were totally compatible with my vegan / ecological philosophy. If you come across others, please let me know.

Sound track

Every trip, every adventure, every experience, should be accompanied by the right music, a soundtrack which adds that touch of magic. I don't recommend walking around New York with headphones on; you don't want to block out the sounds of the city's streets which create a music of their own. Instead, I recommend you listen to the playlist while you are reading this guide or while you are travelling, to ease you into the unmistakable atmosphere of the Big Apple before you arrive. Here is my personal musical tribute to New York City

You can find the playlist, "Passeggiando tra Street e Avenue", on Spotify using this QR code.

1. **Empire State of Mind (Part II) Broken Down** - Alicia Keys
2. **Living For The City** - Stevie Wonder
3. **Walk on the Wild Side** - Lou Reed
4. **Across 110th Street** - Bobby Womack
5. **Theme From New York, New York** - Remastered - Frank Sinatra
6. **New York State of Mind** - Billy Joel
7. **Autumn In New York** - Billie Holiday
8. **Greenwich Village Folk Song Salesman** - Nancy Sinatra
9. **New York Groove** - Ace Frehley
10. **A Heart In New York** - Live at Central Park, NY - Simon & Garfunkel
11. **Everybody's Talkin'** - From "Midnight Cowboy" - Harry Nilsson
12. **Downtown** - 64 Original Release With Petula Clark - Petula Clark
13. **Rockaway Beach** - Remastered Version - Ramones
14. **New York** - Cat Power
15. **Positively 4th Street** - Bob Dylan
16. **New York** - St. Vincent
17. **Chelsea Hotel #2** - Leonard Cohen
18. **No Sleep Till Brooklyn** - Beastie Boys
19. **Uptown Girl** - Billy Joel
20. **New York** - Ja Rule
21. **Englishman In New York** - Sting
22. **New York, I Love You But You're Bringing Me Down** - LCD Soundsystem
23. **The Rising** - Bruce Springsteen
24. **My Way** - Frank Sinatra
25. **Ain't That A Kick In The Head** - 1997 - Remastered - Dean Martin
26. **Let's Fall In Love** - Diana Krall
27. **The Only Living Boy in New York** - Simon & Garfunkel
28. **New York City Cops** - The Strokes
29. **Talkin' New York** - Bob Dylan
30. **Angel Of Harlem** - U2
31. **Manhattan** - Ella Fitzgerald
32. **New York City Serenade** - Bruce Springsteen
33. **53rd & 3rd** - Ramones
34. **I Love New York** - Madonna
35. **First We Take Manhattan** - Leonard Cohen
36. **N.Y. State of Mind** - Nas
37. **New York City Boy** - Pet Shop Boys
38. **Leaving New York** - R.E.M.

Jazz and Broadway

New York has two musical souls: Broadway and Jazz which migrated to the city from New Orleans.

Broadway is famous all over the world for its shows and although the hits come and go, many run for years. The choreography is amazing, the music unforgettable and the scenery mind-blowing. If you want to take in a show or two, remember to book early to get the best places. You can usually find last minute tickets on Broadway, but you may have to settle for mediocre seats. The most popular shows sell out as soon as tickets go on sale. The most famous long-runners are:

- **Cats**, the craziest show you can imagine. If you love the poetry of T S Eliot or if you love cats, this is the show for you; at Neil Simon Theater (250 W 52nd Street).

- **Chicago**, perhaps the most famous show of all, and certainly the most sensual, at the Ambassador Theater (219 W 49th Street).

- **The Lion King**, one of the most spectacular shows ever, at Minskoff Theater (200 W 45th Street).

- **The Phantom of the Opera**, the show with the most performances on Broadway, it has had numerous runs over the years; at the Majestic Theater (245 W 44th Street).

Besides the long running shows, there are many others. One of the latest is Wicked, at the Gershwin Theater (222 W 51st Street), or there is Aladdin, which like The Lion King is a Disney production, at the New Amsterdam Theater (214 W 42nd Street). If you like musicals, you will be spoilt for choice; Broadway has nineteen theaters all offering shows of the highest quality.

If you have a particular show in mind, it's better to book in advance, either on the theater website or using a third party seller like TicketNetwork (https://www.ticketnetwork.com), but if you are easy about what you see and want a good deal, I recommend the TKTS booths which sell same day tickets with a discount of up to 50%. Be prepared to queue.

There are two TKTS booths, one on Broadway, at W 47th Street, under the red steps at Times Square, and one Downtown, on the corner of Front Street and John Street, at South Street Seaport; the second usually has shorter lines.

The other musical soul of the city is jazz. Over the years, clubs have come and gone, some high class, others more run down, but all with a vibe that only jazz can give.

In the 1920s New York exported jazz to the world. These days there are numerous bars and clubs where you can listen to jazz. Here are some of the most evocative, where you can still breathe the soul of jazz.

- Where else to start but Harlem, the beating heart of New York's jazz scene? I recommend **Marjorie Eliot's Jazz** (555 Edgecombe Avenue) especially on a Sunday afternoon, when you can listen to a jam session. Entrance is free, but you can leave a gratuity if you like.

- **Birdland Jazz Club** (315 W 44th Street), near Times Square, jam sessions and good food.

- **Blue Note Jazz Club** (131 W 3rd Street), one of the more sophisticated clubs and also one of the more expensive, but worth a visit for jazz enthusiasts who want to hear some of the best jazz and blues artists in New York.

- **Dizzy's Club Coca Cola**, worth a visit for its views of Columbus Circle and Central Park alone; a

relative newcomer to New York's jazz scene but no less worthy than some of the older clubs. At 10 Columbus Circle.

- **Jazz Standard** (166 E 27th Street), good food at good prices. Entrance is free and there is no obligation to buy drinks or food.
- **Smoke Jazz Club** (2751 Broadway), candlelit tables and traditional decor, a perfect atmosphere for getting in the mood for jazz.
- **Village Vanguard**, at 178 Seventh Avenue South, in the heart of the Village; a modest place where you can hear pure and original jazz.

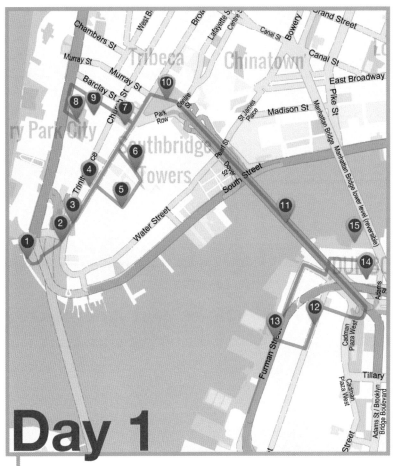

Statue of Liberty and Ellis Island, Federal Reserve, Wall Street, One World Trade Center, Brooklyn

1 NYC Subway: Line 1, South Ferry or Lines 4 and 5, Bowling Green

Begin you trip where everything started – the site of the earliest Dutch settlements and the first houses built in New York – the area now known as Lower Manhattan.

Over the years millions of immigrants to New York have gazed at the Statue of Liberty as they prepared to embark on a new life. To visit the statue take a ferry from **Battery**

56

Park, accessible via subway (Lines 1, 4 and 5).

If you prefer not to visit Liberty Island, take the free **Staten Island Ferry** for great views of the statue. The ferry runs twenty-four hours a day, seven days a week between Manhattan and Staten Island; there's also a café on board. Take a 1 or a 2 train to South Ferry, or an R or a W to Whitehall St and take the ferry from Whitehall Ferry Terminal. The best views are from the back of the boat so go up the first set of stairs and face the terminal. If the doors are closed, push them open; I only understood this after a local told me to use a bit of force.

When you get to Staten Island, get off and take the next ferry back to Manhattan, this time moving to the front of the boat for the best views.

The Statue of Liberty is 93 meters tall, from ground to torch tip, and was a gift from the French people to the American people to mark 100 years of American Independence. It has stood on Liberty Island since 1886 and was restored in 1986 when the original iron frame was replaced with stainless steel; the whole statue is covered in copper, which gives the statue its famous green color (originally the copper was brown, but the process of oxidation has turned it green).

It was once possible to climb up inside the torch, but after the Black Tom explosion in 1916 (an act of sabotage carried out by German agents which damaged the statue's arm) the torch was closed. The original torch was replaced in 1986 during renovation work and is now housed in the museum at the statue's base.

It is possible to climb up inside the crown, but you have to book several months in advance, directly from the park's website (https://www.statueoflibertytickets.com).

Catching the ferry from Liberty Island you can also visit **Ellis Island**, the United States' busiest immigration inspection point for over 30 years. The island now houses the Immigration Museum whose entrance is included in the price of the ferry ticket, as is the entrance to the base of the Statue of Liberty.

Use the computer database to look up the names of your ancestors who may have been processed here when they emigrated to America.

It was only third-class passengers who came through Ellis Island, the more affluent immigrants were controlled on board ship and allowed to disembark directly in New York City.

When you get back to Battery Park, head to **Castle Clinton**, which is the only still intact fort on Manhattan that can be visited; there are other historical forts on Liberty Island, Ellis Island and Governors Island. Today Castle Clinton is the ticket office for the Statue of Liberty and Ellis Island.

2 A little further on is Alexander Hamilton Custom House, which houses the **National Museum of the Native American Indian**. The museum is free and well worth a visit but if you are pushed for time, you can at least admire the building from the outside before moving on.

③ Continue along Broad Street and then Beaver Street to arrive on Broadway; from here you can access New York's oldest public park, **Bowling Green**, built in 1733, next to the site of the original Dutch fort of New Amsterdam.

In the northern end of the park you can find the **Charging Bull Statue**, symbol of the might and resistance of the American people. The statue, by Arturo di Modica, was originally placed in front of the New York Stock Exchange in December 1989 in an act of guerilla art but was moved to its current position because the financial elite of New York were not overly impressed by it (they called the police!).

④ Continuing north we arrive at **Trinity Church** built in 1846.

⑤ Further on is **Wall Street** and **Federal Hall**, where George Washington was inaugurated as the first president of The United States in 1789.

6. To get to the **Federal Reserve Bank of New York** follow William Street until you reach Liberty Street. The building also houses a museum; admission is free, but you need to book well in advance. The ticket includes entrance to the Fed's Gold Vault. (https://app.newyorkfed.org/tours/challenge. jsp).

7. Heading towards the World Trade Center is **St. Paul's Chapel**, famous for providing a point of refuge for the recovery workers after the terrorist attacks of 11th September. Exiting from the opposite side of the church you arrive at the **National September 11 Memorial & Museum**, without a

doubt one of the most moving stops on our tour. The monument's two waterfalls are positioned exactly where the Twin Towers once stood; the names of the victims of the 2001 attack are inscribed around the perimeter together with those of the 1993 terrorist attack on the World Trade Center; you may see some flowers next to some of the names - park officials mark the birthdays of those who died in this way.

A Callery pear tree, known as the **Survivor Tree**, grows in the memorial grounds. In October 2001, the severely damaged tree was discovered at Ground Zero, with snapped roots and burned and broken branches. The tree was removed from the rubble and placed in the care of the New York City Department of Parks and Recreation. After its recovery it was replanted in the Memorial as a symbol of rebirth. Take a moment to sit under its shady and reassuring branches. A visit to the **9/11 Museum** is an experience that you will never forget. Make sure you take your time. Descending to the foundations of the WTC, you can see remains of the Twin Towers and artefacts recovered in the aftermath of the attack. Buy tickets on the museum's website (https://www.911memorial.org).

After visiting the museum you could do some shopping at **Outlet Century 21**, or go up **Freedom Tower** to the One World Trade Center Observatory where you can look down on Lower Manhattan, Brooklyn and the Statue of Liberty and, indeed, the whole of New York. (https://oneworldobservatory.com/).

9 At this point, as you are in the heart of Lower Manhattan, I suggest you head for the World Trade Center's Transportation Hub and admire Calatrava's **Oculus**. The Spanish architect's wonderful glass and steel structure which houses the station is worth taking in from the outside and the inside. When you are ready, take the subway to Brooklyn Heights where we finish our first day of sightseeing.

10 If you are not particularly tired cross **Brooklyn Bridge** on foot starting from **New York City Hall** to arrive at **Brooklyn Heights**; or from Oculus take an R to Court St (about 20 minutes) and take a short walk to Brooklyn Bridge Park from where you can enjoy the best views of New York's skyline . If you are here at sunset you can watch the lights of New York's skyscrapers being switched on as the evening descends over the city.

Brooklyn Bridge was opened on the 25th of May 1883, after 14 years of construction. It was designed by John Roebling, one of the few engineers capable of such an undertaking at the time. Roebling never lived to see his masterpiece completed because he died of tetanus following an accident in which his foot was crushed. His son Washington took over but contracted the bends during construction. He managed to finish the project by supervising the work using binoculars from his house in Brooklyn Heights, and communicating with the engineers through his wife, Emily. Her contribution is commemorated by a plaque on the bridge.

Brooklyn Heights is one of the most historically important areas of New York. It has some 600 houses dating from the Civil War period. Wander around the streets to get a feel of this epoch.

12 One of the most beautiful streets in Brooklyn Heights is Orange Street, where you can admire **Plymouth Church School**, built on the corner of Hicks Street. Inside there is a statue of the abolitionist, Henry Ward Beecher and next to it, a statue of Lincoln.

If you go down Hicks Street to Middagh Street and the corner of Willow Street, you can admire a beautiful wooden house dating from 1824.

13 Take Clark Street towards the river and the Promenade from where you can gaze back at Manhattan and New York Harbor.

From here, make your way to **DUMBO** (Down Under Manhattan Bridge Overpass). This neighborhood, until recently a little rundown and a little seedy, is now one of the trendiest places in New York. There is a buzzing night life, a park and an exciting mix of artists, tech workers and tourists.

Pebble Beach

14 From here head to **Washington Street** where you can relive one of the most famous scenes in cinema history from Sergio Leone's "Once Upon a Time in America" - the Empire State Building framed by the arch of Manhattan Bridge.
Take an F train back to Manhattan.

15 If you are not quite ready to go back to your hotel, stop at **Pebble Beach** and enjoy a bite to eat in the open-air and gaze at the two most famous bridges in New York

Day 1 Lunch:

Whole Foods Market

270 Greenwich St,
New York 10007
tel: +1 212-349-6555
www.wholefoodsmarket.com

Terri
100 Maiden Ln,
New York 10038
tel: +1 212-742-7901

**The Cinnamon Snail
in City Acres Market**
70 Pine Street, 70 Pine St,
New York 10270
tel: +1 917-261-4530
www.cinnamonsnail.com

Beyond Sushi
70 Pine St,
New York 10005
tel: +1 917-261-4530
www.beyondsushinyc.com

Buddha Bodai
5 Mott St,
New York 10013
tel: +1 212-566-8388
www.bodai.com

Day 1 Dinner:

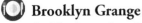 **Brooklyn Grange**

63 Flushing Ave, Brooklyn, NY 11205
tel: +1 347-670-3660
www.brooklyngrangefarm.com

 Peas & Pickles

55 Washington St, Brooklyn, NY 11201
tel: +1 718-488-8336
www.dumbo.is

Juliana's

19 Old Fulton St, Brooklyn, NY 11201
tel: +1 718-596-6700
www.julianaspizza.com

 Sweetgreen

50 Washington St, Brooklyn, NY 11201
tel: +1 347-757-4900
www.sweetgreen.com

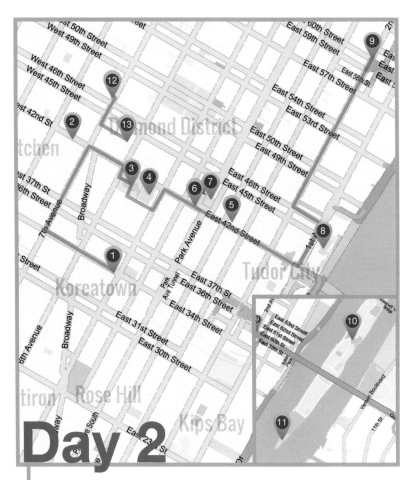

Day 2

Empire State Building, Public Library, Grand Central Terminal, United Nations, Roosevelt Island, Times Square.

1 NYC subway: N, Q, R and W, 34th Street-Herald Sq Station, or B, D, F and M, 34th Street-Herald Sq Station.

The **Empire State Building** is the world's most famous skyscraper and thousands of people visit it every day. My advice is to go early to avoid the queues. A visit, including buying your ticket, taking the elevator, enjoying the views and returning to street level takes the best part of two hours. You can save time by buying tickets online before you go.

http://www.esbnyc.com/it

When it was built the skyscraper was ahead of its time and remains so. Since 1976 the building's lights have maintained a tradition of changing color to recognize various occasions and organizations throughout the year. In 2012, the ownership installed a new computer driven LED light system capable of displaying arrays of different colors which can change instantaneously. Between 1931 and 1967, the skyscraper was the tallest building in the world at 443 meters. It was built in record time (410 days!), was the first building with more than 100 floors and was the first skyscraper to star in a Hollywood blockbuster when it was immortalized in the classic movie, King Kong.

From the Observation Deck on the 86th floor you get a splendid view of the city. Part of the deck is open-air, protected by metal rails, so you can take photos without reflections from glass or other obstacles. The highest observation deck, on the 102nd floor, isn't open-air but you can still get great photos.

2 When you get back to street level you could head to **Madame Tussauds** on 42nd Street between 7th and 8th Avenue. If you want to see the waxwork museum, count on at least an hour and a half for your visit.

3 Otherwise, walk up Fifth Avenue to **Bryant Park** the most elegant of New York's parks where you can play chess or ping pong or take a ride on the carousel.

The park is named after the romantic poet William Cullen Bryant, editor of the New York Evening Post. You can find a statue of him in the park. The area that is now Bryant park has had a chequered history: in the 1800s it was a cemetery and in the 1970s a haunt of drug dealers and petty criminals. It was closed in the 1980s for renovation, when New York was trying to clean up its streets, and reopened as the city was becoming more visitor friendly. Lots of New Yorkers and tourists stop here for lunch and there are regular events and exhibitions. If you are here at Christmas, there is a festive market.

Next to the park is the United States' second biggest public library, the **New York Public Library** on Fifth Avenue at 42nd Street.

The library is a Beaux-Arts masterpiece, whose entrance is guarded by two gigantic lions.

Entrance to the library is free and except for certain reserved areas, tourists can visit the entire building. There are 4 floors:
- on the ground floor in the Children's Center is the original Winnie the Pooh given to Christopher Robin in 1921.
- on the first floor there are rooms containing various archives, such as the Lionel Pincus and Princess Firyal Map Division with over 43,000 maps, the Microform Reading Room with over 350,000 microfilm reels, and the DeWitt Wallace Periodical Room.
- on the second floor is the Jill Kupin Rose Gallery with an exhibition of photographs, texts, objects, and videos illustrating the history, collections, services, and users of New York Public Library.
- on the third floor there are numerous reading rooms and the Bill Blass Public Catalog Room with access to library computers.

The library hosts cultural events and exhibitions throughout the year.

⑤ Having finished your visit of the Library follow 42nd Street to the **Chrysler Building**, my favorite skyscraper. When it opened in 1930, at 319 meters, it was for a short time the tallest building in the world (the Empire State Building opened a few months later). The entrance is at 405 Lexington Ave, between 42nd and 43rd Street; the nearest subway station is the busy Grand Central – 42nd St, lines 4, 5, 6, 7 and S.

The Chrysler doesn't have a viewing deck but if you can, take a peek at the lobby. Remember the building is private so be discreet if you want to steal a few photos.

The skyscraper is classic Art Deco with ceilings in red marble and a vast ceiling painting by Edward Turnbull, Transport and Human Endeavor. The elevators are very beautiful.

Commissioned by Walter Chrysler the building is a homage to the American automobile industry. The spire, in stainless steel, recalls the radiators of Chrysler cars and on the 31st floor there are large car hood ornaments and a frieze of hubcaps and fenders. On the 61st floor there are heads of gargoyle eagles which are a symbol of America.

6 If you are a photographer head to the junction of Vanderbilt Ave and 42nd Street, the best place to photograph the Chrysler Building, before heading to **Grand Central Station**.

7 Grand Central Terminal (also known by the name of the previous station on the same site, Grand Central Station) is a crazy building, perfectly suited to the city it serves. It is the main commuter hub of New York. Long distance intercity trains arrive and depart from Penn Station.

The present building dates from 1913 and its construction was not without controversy as dozens of buildings had to be razed to build it.

Start your visit in the Main Concourse, under the famous clock, a classic meeting place for New Yorkers. Don't forget to look up at the elaborately decorated astronomical ceiling.

Below the Main Concourse is the Dining Concourse where you'll find numerous restaurants including the oldest business operating in the station, the Oyster Bar and Restaurant. Near the Oyster Bar is the Whispering Gallery where the acoustics of the low ceramic arches can cause a whisper to sound like a shout and where two people standing in opposite corners of the entryway, facing the corner, can hear each other above the din of the station. You'll often find couples declaring their love and telling each other their secrets. These aren't the only secrets in the station as underneath Grand Central there are hidden networks of passages and tunnels, including a secret entrance used by F.D. Roosevelt, who wanted to arrive directly to the platforms from the Waldorf Astoria hotel without being bothered by reporters.

8. When you come out of the Grand Central Terminal, head east on 42nd Street until you arrive at the **Headquarters of the United Nations**. There are 45-minute guided tours of the building between 9:00 and 16:30 during which you can learn the history of the United Nations, visit the General Assembly Hall and see various exhibitions. For tickets and information, visit the United Nations website. https://visit.un.org/content/tickets.

Entrance is on 1st Avenue and 45th Street; expect security controls before you enter.

9. If you are not tired you could walk down 1st Avenue or 2nd Avenue to the Roosevelt Island Tramway, an aerial tramway, which connects Roosevelt Island to Manhattan.

If you have an Unlimited Ride MetroCard you can take the tram without paying extra; otherwise buy a ticket. You can also reach Roosevelt Island on an F train and take the aerial tramway back to Manhattan. The views from the aerial tramway are worth seeing at least in one direction.

Roosevelt Island is not on the tourist trail, but it offers an unusual view of the New York Skyline. If you have time visit the lighthouse, where you can sit on a bench or on the grass and get some amazing shots of the river and Upper East Side.

10 **Blackwell House** is the oldest building on the island and the sixth oldest in New York City.

11 On the southern tip of the island is the **Franklin D. Roosevelt Four Freedoms Park** and the ruins of a Smallpox Hospital. The hospital dates from 1856 and a century later was abandoned; it is currently undergoing stabilization work and in the future will be open to the public as a site of historical interest.

12 Take the subway back to Manhattan (1, 2, 3, 7, N, Q, R to 42nd St-Times Square) or the aerial tram and on foot along E 60th Street turning left onto Fifth Avenue then right onto W 47th Street. It's time to visit Times Square. The square is most impressive at night with its neon signs and dazzling lights: wander into some of the shops and then stroll along Broadway, the theater district of New York. Who knows you might even bump into a famous actor.

⑬ The oldest theater on Broadway is the **Belasco Theatre** between Sixth and Seventh Avenue at 111, 44th Street.

Times Square is at the intersection between Seventh Avenue and Broadway and includes the area between Sixth Avenue and Eighth Avenue and between West 42nd and West 47th Street. It isn't really a square so much as the point of intersection of various streets and the frenetic, modern center of New York City.

Since 1907 on New Year's Eve thousands of people have celebrated the stroke of midnight in Times Square and it has featured in hundreds of films. It was here that the iconic photograph of a marine kissing a nurse in a euphoric celebration of the end of the Second World War was taken on 14th August 1945.

The name "Times Square" dates to 1904 when the subway station was opened, and the first billboards and advertisements appeared. Previously known as Longacre Square the area suffered a period of urban decay until the 1990s when Mayor Rudolph Giuliani led an effort to clean it up and make it more tourist friendly

Bryant Park

Day 2 Lunch:

 Two Boots
 337 Lexington Ave,
New York 10016
tel: +1 212-557-7992
web: www.twoboots.com

Franchia Vegan Cafe
12 Park Ave,
New York 10016
tel: +1 212-213-1001
web: www.franchia.com

Terri
685 3rd Ave,
New York 10017
tel: +1 212-983-2200
web: www.terrinyc.com

 Blockheads Burritos
954 2nd Ave,
New York 10022
tel: +1 212-750-2020
web: www.blockheads.com

 fresh&co
569 Lexington Ave,
New York 10022
tel: +1 212-223-2670
web:www.freshandco.com

 Whole Foods Market
226 E 57th St,
New York 10022
tel: +1 646-497-1222
web: www.wholefoodsmarket.com

Day 2 Dinner:

 fresh&co
 8701, 1211 6th Ave,
New York 10036
tel: +1 212-768-8080
web:www.freshandco.com

by CHLOE.
Rockefeller Center 1 Rockefeller Plaza,
New York 10020
tel: +1 646-453-7181
web: www.eatbychloe.com

 Whole Foods Market
1095 6th Ave,
New York 10036
tel: +1 917-728-5700
web: www.wholefoodsmarket.com

 Blockheads
322 W 50th St,
New York 10019
tel: +1 212-307-7029
web: www.blockheads.com

 Maoz
683 8th Ave,
New York 10036 FF $
tel: +1 212-265-2315
web: www.maozusa.com

 Blossom Du Jour
617 9th Ave,
New York 10036
tel: +1 646-998-3535
web: www.blossomdujour.com

 Two Boots Hell's Kitchen
625 9th Ave, New York 10036
tel: +1 212-956-2668
web: www.twoboots.com

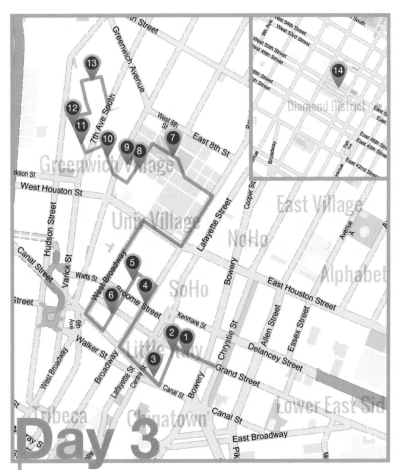

Chinatown, Little Italy, SoHo, Greenwich Village, Rockefeller Center and Top of the Rock at sunset

1 NYC Subway: lines B and D to Grand Street

Today we'll explore some of Manhattan's most interesting neighborhoods - Chinatown, Little Italy, SOHO, the Village and end our day at the Top of the Rock.

We start in **Chinatown**; take the subway (B or D) to Grand Street where you'll be immediately catapulted into New York's Chinese quarter, with its hi-tech shops and typical restaurants. The first Chinese immigrant is said to have arrived here in 1858 establishing himself in Mott Street; in the following years only a trickle of Chinese immigrants came to New York. It wasn't until the 1960s that China town experienced a demographic boom and expanded to the extent that it swallowed a large part of Little Italy. Everywhere you look there are signs, posters, and advertisements in Chinese. Wander through the neighborhood's streets and browse the goods on display. Do some shopping if you like but beware of fakes! Chinatown spreads over Canal Street and Grand Street and the various streets which stretch north towards Little Italy

2 Take Mulberry Street to **Little Italy**, which sadly is past its glory. There are only a few authentic bars and restaurants left; Di Palo's (200 Grand Street) and Ferrara's bakery which makes excellent 'cannoli' for the Feast of San Gennaro (195 Grand Street) still have genuine Italian products as do some of the places on Mulberry Street.

3 Look inside the Catholic **Most Precious Blood Church** where they celebrate traditional mass on San Gennaro's Feast Day on the 19th of September.

Little Italy was once a tight-knit community of Italian immigrants who established themselves here from the second half of the nineteenth century. Incredibly, each Italian region created its own neighborhood. Mulberry Street was home to immigrants from Campania, in Elizabeth Street there were Sicilians (Martin Scorsese was born here) and Mott Street was where families from Calabria and Puglia lived.

Walk down through Little Italy until you arrive at **TriBeCa**, take Broadway northwards and head for one of the most iconic areas of Manhattan, **SoHo** (South of Houston Street). SoHo is famous for its cast-iron architecture and a perfect place to pause and watch people passing by; the buildings are unique and almost all are well preserved and maintained. From TriBeCa you could make a slight detour to 14 N Moore Street to see the Ghostbusters Fire Station.

Browse the boutiques and vintage shops as you stroll through SoHo, and perhaps take a look at some of the modern art galleries (many are in the side streets off Broadway).

④ Perhaps the most beautiful building in SoHo, certainly one of the most architecturally significant, is the **E.V. Haughwout Building** at 488 Broadway on the corner of Broome Street. Take a moment to photograph it before continuing north along Broadway until you reach Spring Street. Turn left and left again into Greene Street where there are more cast-iron masterpieces.

⑤ The **King of Greene Street** is at 72-76 and the **Queen of Greene Street**, a six-story warehouse with a mansard roof, is at 28-30.

⑥ Head south along Greene Street until you reach Canal Street and then turn right to reach W Broadway. The area between Spring Street and Prince Street was once full of art galleries; its heyday was in 1990s but you can still find some interesting exhibitions.

420 West Broadway was the site of the SoHo Gallery Building which exhibited works by Jackson Pollock, Andy Warhol and

Jeff Koons whose scandalous representations of his wife Ilona Staller were displayed here.

7 Follow W Broadway north to Houston Street, turn right and continue until you reach Broadway to arrive at **Greenwich Village**, the ex-Bohemian quarter of New York, where you can still feel a special buzz. The area is home to New York University, one of the largest universities in the USA. Enter the calming and relaxing **Washington Square Park** and mingle with university students and listen to some of the street musicians who often play here.

The park's arch was modelled on the Arc de Triomphe in Paris and was built to commemorate the centennial of George Washington's inauguration. A strange fact - there are thousands of bodies buried beneath the park, which sits atop an ancient potter's field where many indigenous and unknown people were buried. Some say that some of the bodies are those of criminals condemned to hang. In a corner of the park you can see Hangman's Elm which today offers shade to tourists. Near the park's central fountain is a statue of Garibaldi.

8 East of the park is **MacDougal Street**, the main artery of the Village, where you can drop into **Caffè Reggio** at number 119 whose founder introduced Americans to the cappuccino in the 1930s. Inside this historic coffeehouse is the original espresso machine dating from 1902. The cafe was used to film scenes from Godfather II.

9 Keep going south to **Bleecker Street**, once an Italian neighborhood .

10 Here you'll find the **Our Lady of Pompei** church where mass is celebrated once a week in Italian; turn left onto Morton Street, leading to Bedford Street.

11 **Bedford Street** is the most sought-after location in the Village with rents that reflect this. There are many interesting buildings here including the narrowest house in Manhattan at number 75½ which, although only 3 metres wide, has a market value of 4 million dollars!

12 The building you can see on the corner of Bedford Street and Grove Street is in the opening titles to **Friends**.

13 Further on at number 102, on the right, is a Chalet style house once home to Walt Disney.

At the end of the street, turn right to see **Christopher Street**, center of New York's gay rights movement in the 1970s. This colorful neighborhood is full of hip bars and shops, such as the **Magnolia Bakery** on Bleeker Street which sells the most famous cupcakes in Manhattan.

Carrie Bradshaw from Sex and the City lived at number 62 Perry Street.

14 From here take the subway to Midtown, line 1, to 50 St, or B, D, F, M to 47-50 Streets - **Rockefeller Center**. The Rockefeller Center built by the New York magnate is on Fifth Avenue. If you visit at Christmas, you can see the world's most famous Christmas Tree on the Lower Plaza. Inside the Rockefeller Center complex there are shops and restaurants, mainly on the Underground Concourse. Most tourists come to visit the **Top of the Rock Observatory** which has spectacular views over the city. I strongly advise you to buy tickets in advance as the lines can be interminable. The best time to go is at sunset when the light is most suggestive. (https://www.topoftherocknyc.com).

The observatory has three levels and an open terrace with transparent barriers which give views without obstacles. You get a 360° view of the city; look down on Central Park and admire the Empire State Building and the Chrysler Building. The observatory is open from 8am until midnight 365 days a year.

You have probably seen the photograph of construction workers on a metal beam, taken in the 1930s, when the building was being built. Building began in 1931 and only took 2 years thanks to the rapid engineering progress that had been made in preceding decades. The Center is also home to Radio City Music Hall, NBC Studios, MoMa and St. Patrick's Cathedral.

Day 3 Lunch:

Two Boots
201 W 11th St,
New York 10014
tel: +1 212-633-9096
www.twoboots.com

The Butcher's Daughter
581 Hudson St,
New York 10014
tel: +1 917-388-2132
www.thebutchersdaughter.com

Taim West Village
222 Waverly Pl,
New York 10014
tel: +1 212-691-1287
www.taimfalafel.com

Urban | Vegan Kitchen   100% Vegan
41 Carmine St,
New York 10014
tel: +1 646-438-9939
www.urbanvegankitchen.com

Sweetgreen
226 Bleecker St,
New York, NY 10014
tel: +1 917-639-3212
www.sweetgreen.com

Day 3 Dinner:

 **by CHLOE.**
Rockefeller Center 1 Rockefeller Plaza,
New York 10020
tel: +1 646-453-7181
www.eatbychloe.com

fresh&co
8701, 1211 6th Ave,
New York 10036
tel: +1 212-768-8080
www.freshandco.com

Urbanspace
at 570 Lex General Electric Building,
570 Lexington Ave,
New York 10022
tel: +1 917-388-9564
www.urbanspacenyc.com

fresh&co
569 Lexington Ave,
New York 10022
tel: +1 212-223-2670
www.freshandco.com

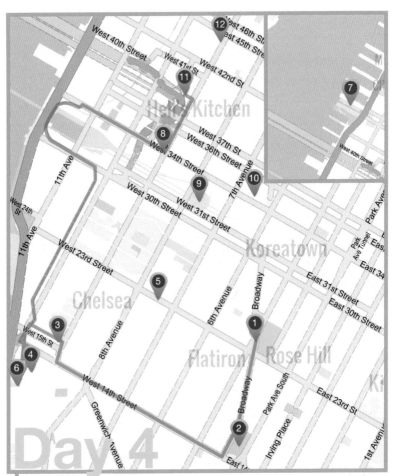

Madison Square Park, Union Square, Chelsea, Meatpacking District and High Line, Hell's Kitchen

1 NYC subway: R and W to Madison Square Park

Madison Square Park is one of New York's most famous parks. It has appeared in countless films and TV shows and gave its name to one of the most famous sporting arenas in the world, Madison Square Gardens. Nearby is the **Flatiron Building**, originally the Fuller Building, which was one of New York's first skyscrapers. Famous for its unmistakable form, it was completed in 1902 and, until the construction of the Park Row Building, was the tallest building in the city (a little difficult to imagine these days!). The vertex of the triangular tower is only two meters across. When the building was erected many New Yorkers were convinced it would blow down, but it is still here.

2 Continue for a few minutes along Broadway to **Union Square** where on Mondays, Wednesdays, Fridays and Saturdays there is the Union Square Greenmarket, a genuine farmers market in the center of the city.

Even if you don't catch the market the square is full of cafes and shops and is a great place to take a break.

3 From Union Square head west on 14th Street until you hit 9th Avenue. Turn right and go into **Chelsea Market**, in front of Google's New York office.

If you prefer, you can get there via subway; take an A, C or E train, or a 1, 2 or 3 to 14th Street/8th Avenue.

The site of Chelsea Market was once a National Biscuit

Company (Nabisco) factory, where Oreo biscuits were invented and first produced. The building is now a covered market but you can still see touches of its industrial past.

The whole of Chelsea is a mix of industry and art, of red brick buildings and modern architecture, full of cafes and fashionable shops. The area declined somewhat after many of its factories closed but it is now a buzzing and vibrant part of the city especially in the evening.

The historical **Meatpacking District** is nearby. This is another area that has completely transformed in recent years and is full of hip places where you can chill. The area hit rock bottom in the 1960s when it was a haunt of drug dealers but since the 1990s it has been totally revamped.

5 If you want you can take a detour to visit the **Chelsea Hotel** (222 West 23rd Street) where Kerouac finished "On The Road", Sid Vicious in all likelihood killed Nancy Spungen (he died of an overdose before the trial) and where Bob Dylan, Patti Smith and Charles Bukowski, among others, encamped. You could then head further south into Greenwich Village with its 19th century houses, market and the iconic Stonewall Inn, site of the Stonewall riots, a turning point for gay rights in America.

6 When you come out of Chelsea Market take 9th Avenue onto Gansevoort Street (one of the trendiest streets on the planet) and head towards the **High Line** which you can access at the junction of Washington Street and Gansevoort Street.

The High Line Park is built on an old elevated railway line which was opened in the 1930s and abandoned in 1980. The railway originally went as far as Spring Street but the southernmost section was demolished in the 1960s. The remaining viaduct escaped demolition but fell into disrepair until a group of local residents and urban explorers, headed by Joshua David and Robert Hammond, began to campaign for its preservation in the 1990s. By then nature had reclaimed the disused space and wild grasses and rugged trees had colonized the tracks. The idea of opening the line as a public park began to take shape. Money for redevelopment began to arrive after the 9/11 terrorist attacks; in part from NYC, in part from Federal Government and in part from donations to "Friends of the High Line". The route was completed in stages between 2009 and 2015 and is maintained by a non-profit organization.

This out of the ordinary park extends over approximately 2,5 km with unbelievable views of the Empire State Building, the streets of Manhattan and New Jersey, it's unlike anything I have ever experienced.

Besides the entrance at Gansevoort Street in the Meatpacking District near the Whitney Museum, you can enter the High Line at 10 other points. The end of the line in the north is at

W 34th Street, on the edge of Hell's Kitchen.
I advise you to walk the whole line as the park's botanical creativeness, works of art and unique views are outstanding.

7 Exit the High Line at W 34th Street. From here you could go north on 11th Avenue, turning left onto West 46th Street to visit the **Intrepid Sea-Air-Space Museum** which showcases an aircraft carrier, a missile submarine and a space shuttle. As an alternative, you could take a cruise on the Circle Line which leaves from Pier 83.

Before (or after) heading for Hell's Kitchen I advise you to check out:

8. **B&H** (420 9th Avenue) the largest non-chain photo and video store in the US with unbeatable prices.

9. **Madison Square Garden** (4 Pennsylvania Plaza), New York's world-famous indoor arena.

B&H

10. And obviously **Macy's** (151 W 34th Street), where the dedicated shopper could easily spend a whole day.

Near Madison Square Garden, is The Pennsy Food Hall, a great place for dinner, with good prices and good food with vegan options.

And now, **Hell's Kitchen**, for many years a gritty working-class neighborhood with a concentration of Irish-Americans. Once the stalking ground of gangs (this was real West Side Story territory) the area was off-limits for tourists. It has gentrified since the 1990s and is now a welcoming and fashionable area of New York with many shops and bars.

This Midtown quarter is west of 8th Avenue, between 34th Street and 57th Street. Superhero fans will recall that the movie Daredevil is set here.

11 If you are here on a Saturday or Sunday between 7.00 and 19.00 I recommend you visit the **Hell's Kitchen Flea Market** (408-424 W 39th Street) with more than 170 stalls. In the evening the area is a great place to eat.

12 9th Avenue has restaurants from all over the world; **Rudy's Bar** has good beer and free hot dogs (for non-vegans!).

High Line

High Line

Day 4 Lunch:

Beyond Sushi Chelsea Market
75 9th Ave,
New York 10011
tel: +1 212-929-2889
www.beyondsushinyc.com

Sweetgreen
32 Gansevoort St,
New York, NY 10014
tel: +1 646-891-5100
www.sweetgreen.com

Benny's Burritos
113 Greenwich Ave,
New York 10014
tel: +1 212-633-9210
www.blockheads.com

Day 4 Dinner:

The Cinnamon Snail
2 Pennsylvania Plaza,
New York, NY 10121
tel: +1 917-261-4530
www.cinnamonsnail.com

fresh&co
363 7th Ave,
New York 10001
tel: +1 212-333-7374
www.freshandco.com

fresh&co
1359 Broadway,
New York 10018
tel: +1 212-253-7374
www.freshandco.com

Beyond Sushi 100% Vegan
134 W 37th St,
New York 10018
tel: +1 212-564-0869
www.beyondsushinyc.com

Sweetgreen
1384 Broadway,
New York, NY 10021
tel: +1 212-334-3020
www.sweetgreen.com

Maoz Falafel & Grill
558 7th Ave,
New York 10018
tel: +1 212-777-0820
www.maozusa.com

Blossom Du Jour 100% Vegan
617 9th Ave,
New York 10036
tel: +1 646-998-3535
www.blossomdujour.com

Two Boots Hell's Kitchen
625 9th Ave,
New York 10036
tel: +1 212-956-2668
www.twoboots.com

Metropolitan Museum of Art, Central Park, Midtown East, Fifth Avenue

1 NYC subway: C, B to 81St-Museum of Natural History or 4, 5 to 86 St Lexington Av or 6 to 77 St

Vegans and animal rights campaigners may have some reservations about the Museum of Natural History but if you choose to visit it there is a guide at the end of today's itinerary. You may prefer to spend extra time in the **Metropolitan Museum of Art**, on Fifth Avenue at number 1000, 82nd Street, the most important museum in New York. The museum has nineteen collections with over two million exhibits. The Egyptian collection is outstanding and the European and American collections are vast.

The "Met" also houses many African, Asian, Byzantine, Islamic and Oceanic artworks and artefacts, including musical instruments, arms and armor, clothes and jewelry as well as presenting reconstructions of various environments from the past.

If you have limited time or if you are overwhelmed and can't decide where to begin, here is a quick guide:

- First Floor and Mezzanine:

Galleries 100 to 138 Egyptian Art

Galleries 150 to 176 Greek and Roman Art

Galleries 300 to 307 Medieval and Byzantine Art

Galleries 350 to 358 American, Asian and Oceanic Art

Galleries 500 to 556 European Art

Galleries 700 to 774 American Art

Galleries 813, 828, 829 and 830 Modern and Contemporary Art

Galleries 950 to 962 Robert Lehman Collection

- Second and third floor:

Galleries 200 to 253 Asian Art

Galleries 400 to 406 Near and Middle Eastern Art

Galleries 450 to 464 Islamic Art

Galleries 600 to 644 European Paintings

Galleries 680 to 684 Musical Instruments

Galleries 690 to 693 Drawings and Prints

Galleries 800 to 827 European Paintings and Sculptures

Galleries 850 to 852 Photography

- Third floor:

Galleries 900 to 925 Modern and Contemporary Art

- Ground floor:

Galleries 980 to 981 The Costume Institute

For more information about the various collections consult the museum website https://www.metmuseum.org. Some exhibitions may vary throughout the year.

If you have time and are into medieval art, I recommend **The Cloister Center of Medieval Art**, a separate branch of the Met in northern Manhattan's Fort Tyron Park; entrance is included in the ticket to the Met on Fifth Avenue. If you are uncomfortable with animals being used for entertainment purposes, be aware that the museum sometimes stages performances with live animals.

The Cloisters museum and gardens provide an evocative backdrop for an impressive collection of European art mainly from the Gothic and Romanesque periods.

The museum is centered around four medieval cloisters, dismantled in France and relocated to New York. The Saint Giulheim Cloister is from a Benedictine monastery in Saint-Guilhem-le-Désert dating from 804, the Cuxa Cloister was from an Abbey on Mount Canigou dating from 878, the Trie Cloister was compiled mainly from the convent at Trie-sur-Baïse, and the Bonnefont Cloister comprises of parts from a number of French abbeys, mainly the 12th century Abbaye de Bonnefont.

To get there, take an A train to Dyckman Street.

If there is still enough daylight when you come out of the Met you could explore Central Park, the green heart of the city and a world unto itself.

② Before you lose yourself in the park take a look at the **Dakota Building** on the NW corner of 72nd Street and Central Park. Commissioned by Edward S. Clark West, head of the Singer Manufacturing Company, its name reflects the remoteness of this part of New York at the time (Dakota territory was considered an untamed outpost of the United States).

The building has had many famous residents and in December 1980 John Lennon was murdered at the south entrance.

Note the building's wide entrance designed for carriages and horses; inside there were also stables equipped with lifts to transport the carriages to the upper floors.

New York's **Central Park** was opened in 1876 at a cost of 14 million dollars (an inconceivable amount for the time). It stretches from 59th Street to 110th Street, over 50 blocks of green.

In the 1970s the park was emblematic of New York's decadence, a refuge for criminals and drugs dealers. Since then things have completely changed thanks to the foundation of the Central Park Conservancy which has been responsible for reclaiming, cleaning and restructuring the park.

It's difficult to know what to advise you to visit in Central Park; I love nothing more than getting disorientated and finding myself in an area I have never visited before. One tip – if you get completely lost, look at the lampposts. Every lamp has four numbers at its base, the first two tell you the nearest street and the last two whether you are nearest to the east or west side of the park (even numbers mean east, odd numbers mean west).

Here are some of the park's most famous sites. Get a map at one of the entrances or install one of the Apps available to help you navigate, as finding them without can be quite an adventure!

3 **Strawberry Fields**: dedicated to the memory of John Lennon. The memorial was funded by Yoko Ono and the mosaic was a gift from the city of Naples.

4 **Belvedere Castle:** the highest point in the park where you can admire the surrounding greenery.

5 **Bow Bridge** and **Bethesda Terrace** and Fountain. The fountain represents an angel blessing the waters of the Pool of Bethesda in Jerusalem. It was commissioned to commemorate the opening of the Croton Aqueduct which provided New York with a dependable supply of fresh water for the first time and helped to protect its inhabitants from the epidemics of cholera that often hit the city.

6 **Jacqueline Kennedy Onassis Reservoir**; a decommissioned reservoir in the heart of the park. If you walk around its edge, make sure you obey the direction arrows, joggers can get very upset if they find walkers going the wrong way!

7 **The Mall,** the only straight path in the park which leads to Bethesda Fountain.

East of the Bethesda Fountain is the **Central Park Model Boat Sailing, Alice in Wonderland** and **Glade Arch**, as well as the **Metropolitan Museum of Art** further north.

Outside the park, at its south west corner, is Columbus Circle where you can photograph the statue of the famous explorer and on Fifth Avenue to the east is the world-famous Plaza hotel.

8 Take East Drive to reach the **Guggenheim Museum** (1071 Fifth Avenue on the Corner of E 89th Street) which is worth seeing from the outside even if you don't have time to see its collections of modern and contemporary art.

9 The northern most reaches of the park mark the beginning of Harlem. Here you can find **Conservatory Garden**, the only formal garden in Central Park, and Harlem Meer. Not far from here is **Huddlestone Arch** which has featured in numerous films and is one of many arches worth seeing, such as **Glen Span Arch**, near The Pool or **Springbanks Arch**, on 102nd St Crossing.

10 Animal lovers will want to see the bronze statue of the canine hero, **Balto**, near the Tisch Children's Zoo, west of East Drive and 67th Street.

11 If you come out of Central Park at **Grand Army Plaza** you are just west of Fifth Avenue, a big spender's paradise. If you are a brand freak or a high-end window shopper, then this is your street. All the way down to the Rockefeller Center there are luxury stores and designer labels. Breakfast at Tiffany's?

12 If you disagree with live animals being used as exhibits, you probably won't want to visit the **Museum of Natural History**. I provide a guide here because it is an incredible museum which seeks to promote environmental campaigns and sustainability. You can choose whether or not you want to see it. There are often long lines at the ticket offices, so I strongly advise you to buy tickets online rather than on the door. (https://www.amnh.org).

If you have kids this is the best museum in New York and there is a lot for adults too. Founded nearly 150 years ago, the museum is as much a part of New York as the Met. It has featured in various films including Night at the Museum. The museum's imposing entrance is reflective of its vast scale and scope; inside there are thousands of exhibits, dioramas and inter-active displays.

One day isn't enough to see everything; below are some of the highlights but even planning to see all of these is ambitious!

- Lower Level: Dorothy and Lewis B. Cullman Hall. Look out for the moonrocks from the Apollo missions; the Ecosystem Sphere and the Willamette meteorite weighing 15.5 tons.

- First Floor: Theodore Roosevelt Memorial Hall which commemorates a side of the ex-president you may not know, that of a keen naturalist and conservationist.

- Bernard Family Hall of North American Mammals with 43 dioramas showing North America's natural history.

- Milstein Hall of Ocean Life with a 30m replica of a blue whale, the biggest animal that has ever existed, as well as models of dolphins and tuna.

- Hall of North American Forests and the 1,400-year-old sequoia tree felled in California in 1891.

- Hall of Northwest Coast Indians where you can see the ceremonial masks used by the Kwakiutl people and the weapons and armor of native Americans from the northwest coast.

- Lucy, the woman who lived 3.18 million years ago whose skeleton was found in 1974 by researchers. She is named after the Beatles song, Lucy in the Sky with Diamonds (Anne and Bernard Spitzer Hall of Human Origins).

- The Patricia Emerald, one of the largest ever found, unearthed in Colombia in 1920.

- The Harriet and Robert Heilbrunn Cosmic Pathway, a 100m-long path that winds its way from the Big Bang through the 13 billion years of the Universe's history (Rose Center for Earth and Space).

- Scales of the Universe in the Rose Center for Earth and Space that puts into perspective the smallest to the largest things in the universe, from microorganisms to planets.

- The Hayden Planetarium, a sphere with a diameter of more than 25 meters, whose top half houses the Star Theater which projects high resolution "space shows" of dust clouds, galaxies and constellations (Rose Center for Earth and Space).

- Second Floor: Barosaurus, the skeleton of the plant-eating dinosaur (Theodore Roosevelt Rotunda).

- The Akeley Hall of African Mammals, containing 28

dioramas of African mammals including zebras, giraffes, gazelles, elephants, lions and rhino.
- The Hayden Big Bang Theater, a multimedia reconstruction of the Big Bang.
- **Third Floor:** Hall of Reptiles and Amphibians; check out the Galapagos giant tortoise.
- Folsom Spear Point in the Hall of Eastern Woodland Indians which is 10,000 years old. When it was found in the 1920s it challenged the accepted timeframe of human migration into North America which was thought to have been much later.
- The huge stone human figures or moai from Easter Island (Rapa Nui) in the Margaret Mead Hall of Pacific Peoples.
- **Fourth Floor:** Tyrannosaurus rex, Deinonychus and Apatosaurus, unearthed at the end of the nineteenth century in the Hall of Saurischian Dinosaurs.
- The Glen Rose Trackway, the 107-million-year-old dinosaur footprints found in Texas, Hall of Saurischian Dinosaurs.
- The duckbilled dinosaur mummy from the Mesozoic era, the Triceratops skeleton, Anatotitan and Stegosaurus in the Hall of Ornithischian Dinosaurs.
- the Warren Mastodon, found in 1845, 11,000 years old and one of the most complete mastodon skeletons known (Paul and Irma Milstein Hall of Advanced Mammals).
- Mammoth skeleton, also 11,000 years old (Paul and Irma Milstein Hall of Advanced Mammals).

Bethesda Terrace and Fountain

Day 5 Lunch:

 Whole Foods Market
10 Columbus Circle Ste Sc101,
New York 10019
tel: +1 212-823-9600
www.wholefoodsmarket.com

 Blossom Du Jour Express
1000S 8th Ave,
New York 10019
tel: +1 212-765-6500
www.blossomdujour.com

 fresh&co
200 W 57th St,
New York 10019
tel: +1 212-513-7374
www.freshandco.com

 Sweetgreen
311 Amsterdam Ave,
New York, NY 10023
tel: +1 212-496-4081
www.sweetgreen.com

 Blossom on Columbus
507 Columbus Ave,
New York 10024
tel: +1 212-875-2600
www.blossomnyc.com

 fresh&co
1260 Lexington Ave,
New York 10028
tel: +1 212-953-7374
www.freshandco.com

 Sweetgreen
1500 3rd Ave,
New York, NY 10028
tel: +1 646-666-0860
www.sweetgreen.com

Two Boots Upper East Side
1617 2nd Ave,
New York 10028
tel: +1 212-734-0317
www.twoboots.com

Candle 79
154 E 79th St,
New York 10075
tel: +1 212-537-7179
web: www.candle79.com

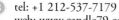

Day 5 Dinner:

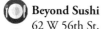

Beyond Sushi
62 W 56th St,
New York 10019
tel: +1 646-964-5097
www.beyondsushinyc.com

Sweetgreen
66 E 55th St,
New York, NY 10022
tel: +1 646-859-0100
www.sweetgreen.com

---

by CHLOE. Rockefeller Center
1 Rockefeller Plaza,
New York 10020
tel: +1 646-453-7181
www.eatbychloe.com

---

fresh&co
8701, 1211 6th Ave, New York 10036
tel: +1 212-768-8080
www.freshandco.com

Urbanspace at 570 Lex
General Electric Building,
570 Lexington Ave, New York 10022
tel: +1 917-388-9564
web: www.urbanspacenyc.com

---

fresh&co
569 Lexington Ave,
New York 10022
tel: +1 212-223-2670
www.freshandco.com

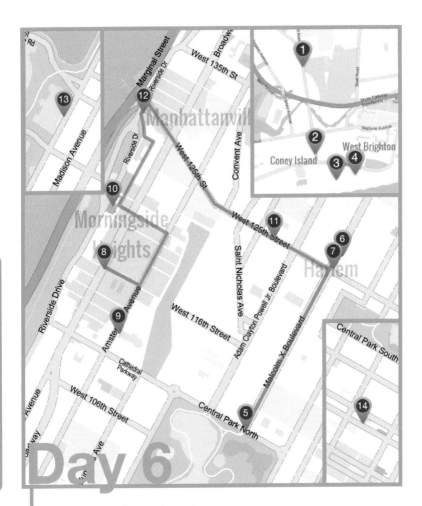

Coney Island, Harlem, Bronx

1 NYC Subway: D, F, N, Q to Coney Island - Stillwell Avenue

Today's itinerary is slightly different, slightly alternative, a little off the classic tourist trails. It includes places where New Yorkers still hang out and where you can live the culture and history of the Big Apple in first person.

First stop is **Coney Island**, the by now rather shabby and melancholy beach area of New York City.

Take an N train to enjoy great views of Brooklyn and its bridge on the ride.

2 **Nathan's Famous Hot Dogs and Restaurants**, near the subway exit, hosts a hotdog eating contest every year on the 4th July. Unsurprisingly, their menu doesn't offer much for vegans.

In the early years of the twentieth century Coney Island was home to three large amusement parks which attracted millions of visitors a year. The resort's golden years lasted until the 1960s when its popularity waned due to competition from more sophisticated forms of entertainment.

3 If you walk along the **Boardwalk** in the summer, you can't avoid mingling with New Yorkers enjoying a day out. You may notice that there are many signs and menus in the Cyrillic alphabet as the area has a large Russian and Ukrainian community.

The ocean here is choppy but, if you are brave enough, it isn't excessively risky for swimmers (swimming is only permitted when there are lifeguards on duty). If you are not keen on getting wet there is a lot else to do.

4 I suggest, **Deno's Wonder Wheel** which opened in1920 and the **Cyclone Rollercoaster** dating from 1927.

After lunch take the subway back uptown, all the way to **Harlem**, one of the most beautiful quarters of the city, soaked in history, where the civil rights movement flowered and where jazz flouted all the rules. The area's dilapidated buildings and street names – Martin Luther King Boulevard, Malcolm X Boulevard, Adam Clayton Powell, Jr. Boulevard – are reminders of the neighborhood's combative past.

The southernmost part of Harlem touches the northern tips of Central Park, while the north is bounded by the Harlem and Hudson Rivers.

The territory, once inhabited by native American tribes, was first a Dutch settlement and then an English village. African Americans arrived in large numbers during the Great Migration as they fled from the Jim Crow South.

The cultural significance of Harlem for New York, for America and for the world from 1918 to the mid 1930s, the years of the "Harlem Renaissance", was immense. The neighborhood gave birth to an intellectual and artistic explosion which rivalled the centuries earlier European Renaissance. Until the 1990s it could be scary to wander around Harlem as a tourist but these days the neighborhood, like the Bronx, is pretty safe.

5 To get to Harlem take a 2 or a 3 train to 110 Street Station – Central Park North. From here you can walk down **Lenox Avenue / Malcom X Boulevard** (the street has two names), the heart of Harlem.

6 Don't miss taking a look at **Sylvia's Restaurant** (328 Malcom X Blvd), the most famous soul food restaurant in New York, although not that great for vegans.

7 The **Red Rooster** a few steps down from Sylvia's offers more modern dishes, but again, vegan diners may be challenged.

8 To visit **Columbia University** (line 1 at 116 Street Station – Columbia University) head west towards the Hudson River on W 123rd Street (a few blocks before the two restaurants)

turning left on Amsterdam Avenue. The university has many famous alumni including Barack Obama, Theodore Roosevelt and Jack Kerouac. It is also where Enrico Fermi taught.

9 Not far from Columbia University is the Cathedral of **St. John the Divine**, on Amsterdam Avenue between W 110th Street and W 113th Street. One of the biggest cathedrals in the world, its constant state of construction and restoration, has earned it the nickname St John the Unfinished.

10 Martin Luther King once preached at the nearby **Riverside Church**, which has an impressive interior and the fourteenth largest organ in the world. The church is west of the university, towards the Hudson at 490 Riverside Drive. You may prefer

to head straight back to Harlem. Retrace your steps along Amsterdam Avenue and right onto 123rd Street. Turn left onto Frederick Douglass Blvd and then right at Martin Luther King Blvd (also called 125th Street), where you can find the iconic Apollo Theatre.

The **Apollo Theatre**, built in 1913-14, boasts a long list of renowned performers including Michael Jackson, Ella Fitzgerald and James Brown.

If you are a Duke Ellington and Fletcher Henderson fan it's worth stopping at the **Cotton Club** on W 125th Street (not the original but a pretty good replacement). It's a bit out of the way, near the Hudson, not far from Riverside Church. After visiting the church, you could walk north alongside or through the park on Riverside Dr. to the club (about 10 minutes), before heading to the Apollo by taking Martin Luther King Blvd / W 125th which starts here.

One of the most uplifting experiences in Harlem is listening to a gospel choir. If you are lucky enough to be in the neighborhood on a Sunday morning you can hear gospel singing in many of its churches. It really is an incredibly uplifting experience for believers and non-believers alike. You can contact the churches directly or take part in an organized gospel tour.

13 After Harlem, you could visit one of the nearby museums such as the **Metropolitan Museum**, at 1000 Fifth Avenue, which houses some of the most important collections of art and artefacts in the world. You could easily spend half a day in each one of its permanent exhibitions, such as the Egyptian Collection (see day 5).

14 Alternatively, you could spend some time at **MoMa** (11 W 53 Street), one of the most important modern and contemporary art museums in the world. The museum has defined and shaped innovations in art over recent decades. It is a must for anyone interested in twentieth and twenty-first century trends in a range of artistic disciplines including architecture, film, photography, sculpture, design and much more.

15 If you are not much of a modern art fan, or if you'd prefer to experience another area of New York, I recommend that you go north to the **Bronx**. For years the Bronx was a realm of criminals and gangs and definitely not a place for tourists. Since the 1980s things have slowly changed with new investments, revitalization projects and community initiatives.

One area in particular is worth a visit, the **Bronx Little Italy**, which is more alive and more genuine than the more famous Italian quarter in Manhattan. The food is as good as it gets and the shops unflashy and friendly.

The Bronx Italian quarter extends along **Arthur Avenue**. Take a D train to Fordham Rd; from here head east down E 188th Street until you get to Flood Triangle Park. Cross 3rd Ave and Washington Ave and continue on E 188th until you reach Arthur Ave where you can immediately sense the Italian atmosphere. There are bars, pizza restaurants and the excellent Belmont Library and Enrico Fermi Cultural Center dedicated to Italian-American culture and heritage. You'll hear people speaking Italian and a version of American

English which owes a lot to the cadences of southern Italian dialects; it's an incredible place.

You can't hope to visit everything the Bronx has to offer in one afternoon or even in one day. Here are some of the Bronx's attractions for you to take your pick.

16 The **Yankee Stadium**, home to the New York Yankees. Not merely a stadium, but a complex with shops, a cinema, gyms, a sports museum, restaurants and cafes.

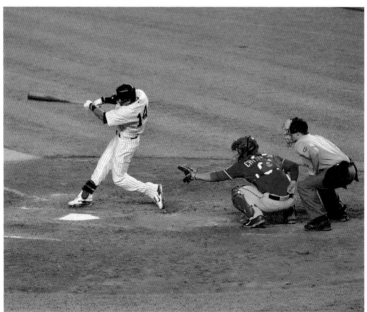

17 The **Rockefeller Fountain**, in the Bronx Zoo, which has a strange history. It was originally intended for a piazza in Como, Italy and was bought by William Rockefeller in 1902 who brought it to New York.

18 **Edgar Allan Poe Cottage**, in Poe Park, where the famous Gothic writer lived.

19 **New York Botanical Garden** with 50 different gardens and plant collections from all over the world. Here there is a waterfall, technically a dam, constructed on the Bronx River originally to power a mill, and 50 acres of never-logged forest, the largest remnant of indigenous pre-European settlement vegetation left in New York.

New York's fourth biggest park, the **Van Cortlandt Park**, is also in the Bronx. It is a beautiful place to be at sunset. If you have time explore the Putnam, Muir and John Kieran trails.

Finally, **Wave Hill**, another splendid public park along the Hudson River with fantastic views of New Jersey.

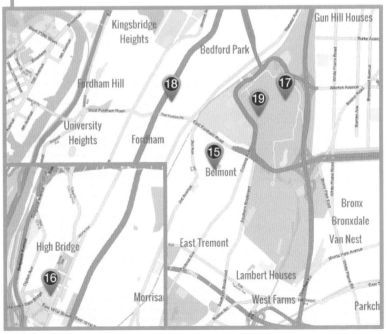

GIOVANNI'S

RESTAURANT & BAR

WOOD BURNING BRICK OVEN PIZZERIA

GIOVANNI'S

...s of Arthur Avenue GIOVANNI'S RESTAURANT BAR & BRICK OVEN PIZZERIA 2343

Giovanni's
BRICK OVEN PIZZA RESTAURANT

Giovanni's
INDOOR & OUTDOOR DINNING IN THE BACK

Bronx Little Italy

Day 6 Lunch:

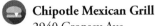

Chipotle Mexican Grill
2940 Cropsey Ave,
Brooklyn, NY 11214
tel: +1 718-266-0380
www.chipotle.com

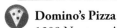

Domino's Pizza
1208 Neptune Ave,
Brooklyn, NY 11224
tel: +1 718-265-5600
www.dominos.com

Footprints cafe
1521 Surf Ave,
Brooklyn, NY 11224
tel: +1 718-265-2530
www.footprintscafenyc.com

Day 6 Dinner:

Whole Foods Market
100 W 125th St,
New York 10027
tel: +1 212-678-1940
www.wholefoodsmarket.com

Seasoned Vegan
55 St Nicholas Ave,
New York 10026
tel: +1 212-222-0092
www.seasonedvegan.com

Uptown Veg
52 E 125th St,
New York, NY 10035
tel: +1 212-987-2660
www.facebook.com/Uptown-Veg-374509442644237

Day 7

Shopping and movie locations
Shopping:

Our last day! Let's cheer ourselves up by going shopping.

If you want to splash out on luxury and designer items the area between 45th and 60th Street on Fifth Avenue and Madison Avenue on Upper East Side is your patch.

For American brands the shops on 34th Street, near Herald Square, where you'll also find the institutional Macy's are good hunting grounds.

Times Square is the realm of souvenirs.

If you what something more alternative you'll find more to suit you in SoHo and the Meatpacking District.

The Century 21 Department Store has some good bargains on sportswear, accessories etc. There are three in New York: Broadway at 1972, Dey Street at number 21 and Cortlandt Street at number 22.

If you want to go further afield check out the Woodbury Outlet Common in Central Valley which has over 200 stores and services. To avoid apocalyptic scenes of consumerism don't go at the weekend. http://www.premiumoutlets.com/outlet/woodbury-common

There are several shuttle buses from Manhattan to the outlet run by private agencies which often offer discount shopping vouchers.

Film and TV Locations:

If you are not much of a shopper, you might want to check out some film and TV locations instead of hitting the shops. Here's my selection:

Many scenes from **Once Upon a Time in America**, Sergio Leone's masterpiece, were shot around DUMBO especially between Washington Street and Water Street from where you can photograph Manhattan Bridge to recapture the frame of the original poster. Take an F to York Street Station.

The famous spot from **Breakfast at Tiffany's**, outside the store on Fifth Avenue, is not difficult to find. The store is next to Trump Tower. Take an F to 57th Street Station.

The glitzy Indian restaurant where Karen and Matt meet in **Daredevil** is exactly like it is in the film. Its name is Panna II Garden and you'll find it at number 93 on 1st Avenue in East Village, take an R or W train to 8th Street Station.

The Nelson & Murdock Law Office is in Williamsburg, Brooklyn at 363 S 4th Street, take an M to Hewes Street Station.

The exterior of the **Friends** house in West Village is easily recognizable between Gove Street and Bedford Street, take a 1, 2 or 5 to Christopher Street. Disappointingly Central Perk café doesn't exist, but you can visit the Pulitzer Fountain in Central Park which features in the show's opening credits.

Ghostbusters was filmed in numerous locations around New York. The unmistakable fire station is in TriBeCa, N Moore Street, lines 1, 2 and 5 to Franklin Street Station.

The library scenes were shot in the New York Public Library, line 7 to 5th Avenue, or lines B, D, F or M to 42th Street Station. Dana Barrett's apartment is in a building off Central Park, between W 65th and 66th Street; you probably passed it when you visited the park, take an A, B, C or D to Columbus Circle.

The famous orgasm scene from **When Harry Met Sally** took place at Katz's Delicatessen, on 205 East Houston Street, line F to Delancey Street or lines J, M and Z to Essex Street Station. The table where Sally and Harry sat is still there.

MacLaren's Pub from **How I met your mother** doesn't exist, but it is based on a real pub, McGee's, at 240 W 55th Street which is full of photos and memorabilia connected to the show. Take line N, Q, R or W to 57th Street Station.

If you visited Coney Island, you may have recognized some locations from **The Warriors**, although sadly, most no longer exist and the area has changed significantly since the film was made in 1979.
If you go to Riverside Park you can still find the Dinosaur Playground where the story begins. Take a 1, 2, 3 or 5 train to 96th Street Station.

The 1992 screwball movie, **Home alone 2: Lost in New York** features many of New York's famous landmarks including Central Park, the Rockefeller Center and the unmistakable Plaza Hotel at 768 on Fifth Avenue, line N, R or W to 5th Ave Station.

Woody Allen's **Manhattan** is a bitter/sweet love-letter to New York. It would be impossible to mention all the film's locations so here are just two: the Boating Lake in Central Park which you probably saw when you visited the park, and the location shown on the movie's original poster with Allen and Keaton on a bench silhouetted against Queensboro Bridge. You can visit the exact spot in Sutton Place Park at East 58th Street. Take an N, R or W train to Lexington Av/59 St, a 4, 5, 6 or 7 to 59 St-Lexington Av Station, a Q to Lexington Av - 63 St Subway Station or an E to Lexington Av-53 St.

The famous skirt blowing scene from **The Seven Year** Itch was filmed on the corner between Lexington Avenue and 52nd Street. There is nothing to distinguish the subway grate where Marylin Monroe stood as her dressed billowed in the upward breeze, apart from the crowds which sometimes gather around it. It's in front of L' Entrecôte, lines 4 and 6 to 51st Street or lines E and M to Lexington Avenue.

New York is the "city" in **Sex and the City** and is as much of a star as the show's human protagonists. I already mentioned Carrie's house at 66 Perry Street which you can reach by taking lines 1, 2 and 5 to Christopher Street Station. Not far from the house is Magnolia Bakery, at 411 Bleecker Street, a favorite pitstop for Carrie and Miranda. The fountain scene during which Carrie finally rejects Aidan was filmed at Columbus Circle, lines A, B, C and D, to Columbus Circle Station.

In the 2002 **Spiderman** movie the Daily Bugle Building is none other than the Flatiron Building, on Fifth Avenue near Madison Square Park, lines R and W to East 23rd Street Station.

As I mentioned, **Night at the Museum** is set at the Museum of Natural History, at the junction of Central Park West and 79th Street. Even if you don't like the film, the museum is one of the best in New York, take lines C and B to 81st Street-Museum of Natural History Station.

Unusual Places:

If you are tired of the usual tourist spots, you could check out some of these less well-known gems. My list is by no means exhaustive as New York has endless possibilities just waiting to be discovered.

New York Transit Museum (at the junction between Boerum Place and Schermerhorn Street) explores the history and evolution of transport in New York. Take a 4 or 5 to Borough Hall. The museum is housed in the now abandoned Court Street subway station and has collections of bus, subway and railway memorabilia from the early 1900s to the present day. You can also visit a section of the old subway track.

Merchant's House Museum, dating from the 1800s, with historical furniture and a ghost. At 29 E 4th Street, take a D or an F to Broadway-Lafayette Street.

The street art on **Bowery Wall** at 76 E Houston Street, lines 4 and 6 to Bleecker Street. Since the 1970s world-famous artists, starting with Keith Harding, have left their mark on the wall which since 2008 has been curated and promoted by Goldman Properties in collaboration with The Hole, an art gallery in SoHo. There is a regular rotation of artists with displays lasting from four to six months. None of the works are permanent so you can see a different work every time you visit New York.

Alice's Tea Cup is a chain of three tea houses (Chapter i, Chapter ii and Chapter iii) inspired by Lewis Carroll's famous book. The tea is brewed to perfection and the atmosphere is delightful. Find them at: Chapter i 102 W 73rd Street, lines 1, 2 and 3 to 72nd St-Broadway; Chapter ii 156 E 64th Street, lines Q and R to Lexington Av-63St Subway or N and R to Lexington Av/59th Street; Chapter iii 220 E 81st Street, lines Q and R to 86th Street.

McSorley's Old Ale House, 15 E 7th Street, lines N, Q and R to 8th Street Station. A real old Irish tavern, opened in 1854, with an atmosphere worthy of the best pubs in Dublin. It's full of intriguing objects and serves one of the best beers in New York.

Dyker Heights (Brooklyn) at Christmas. In a way-over-the-top display of yuletide cheer the neighborhood's homeowners compete to create the gaudiest and most razzle-dazzle Christmas scenes, complete with inflatable snowmen and giant Santas. Take a D train to 79th St or an N or R to 86th St. The best light displays are from 11th Avenue to 13th Avenue and from 83rd Street to 86th Street.

You can take a ferry to **Governors Island** from Battery Maritime Building at 10 South Street which is free on Saturdays and Sundays for the sailings at 10:00, 11:00 and 11:30. You can either hire a bike or explore on foot. The island often hosts special events especially in the summer. There are fantastic views of the Statue of Liberty and Manhattan; although many New Yorkers escape here at the weekend, it is not on the usual tourist itineraries. https://govisland.com

During Prohibition **The Back Room** (102 Norfolk Street, line F to Delancey St) was a "Speakeasy" and it still has the charm of the 1920s. Don't be put off by the hidden entrance, there is no sign on the street, you have to go downstairs and through a door (it wasn't meant to be easy to find!).

Spuyten Duyvil is an upper middle-class area of the Bronx which is well worth exploring. Getting here is quite simple; take line 1 to W 231 St/Broadway. Not far from the station, where the Harlem River meets Spuyten Duyvil Creek, there is the Big C Rock, a sheer rock face on which is painted a 'Big C' in honor of Colombia University. The area has a number of historically interesting houses, perhaps the most beautiful is the Charlotte Bronte Villa at 2501 Palisade Avenue. Netherald Avenue also has some beautiful homes. While you are here, take a stroll through the Henry Hudson Memorial Park and Ewen Park and have a look at the eclectically designed Edgehill Church of Spuyten Duyvil.

Sylvan Terrace, in Washington Heights, is a cobblestone street in the north of Harlem with wooden rowhouses built in 1882. Take line 1 to 157th St. On the top of the hill, in Roger Morris Park, is the Morris-Jamel Mansion dating from 1765, the oldest house in Manhattan. In 1776 George Washington used the house as a temporary headquarters following his army's defeat in the Battle of Long Island and in 1790 he hosted a cabinet dinner here with Thomas Jefferson, John Adams, James Madison Alexander Hamilton and William Knox in attendance.

I advise approaching the house from the west, via St. Nicolas Avenue.

Hoboken, in New Jersey, not only has amazing views of Manhattan from **River Waterfront Walkway**, it is also the neighborhood of Carlo's Bake Shop (owned by Buddy Valastro aka Cake Boss) which is situated in Washington Street. The easiest way to get to Hoboken is to take a PATH train. Two lines connect Hoboken and Manhattan, the Hoboken-33rd Street service and the Hoboken-World Trade Center service.

River Waterfront Walkway

Top of the Rock

Index of Places

Photo Credits

Backcover from left to right: Nix, Little Choch Apothecary, XYST, below Roberto Rossi

Pages 5, 8, 11, 22, 24, 51, 138, 143, 153: Christian Bazzani

Pages 142, 146 Laura Colli Ghisalberti

Pages 59, 63, 64, 90, 115, 129, 134 bottom: Christian Bazzani

Pages 67 bottom: Giacomo Sergi

Pages 7, 133 top: Christian Bazzani

Pages 80, 140 top: Giacomo Sergi

Pages 94, 151: Giacomo Sergi

Page 102 above right: Christian Bazzani

Pages 111, 112, 132 bottom: Metropolitan Museum of Art, New York

Page 130, 146, 148 bottom: Laura Colli Ghisalberti

Page 144 right: Giacomo Sergi

Page 144 bottom: Daniela Loprevite

Page 146: Alice's Tea Cup website

Page 26: Bar Verde

Pages 28, 34: Arata

Page 30: Nix

Page 31: John's of 12th Street

Page 32: Little Choc Apothecary

Page 33: Orchard Grocer

Page 36: Two Boots

Page: 37: Franchia

Page: 38: Terri

Pages 39, 45, 68, 83, 95, 108: photos of restaurants

Page 40 left: ©Brooklyn Grange, www.BrooklynGrangeFarm.com

Pages 69, 84: ©Brooklyn Grange, www.BrooklynGrangeFarm.com

All other photos: Roberto Rossi

In no particular order, I am grateful to:
My wife Barbara, my Mum and Dad, my cats, my parents-in-law Franca
and Enrico, Andrea Schincaglia and Sabrina Cellai and the entire staff
of Reporter Live, Nicola Rossini, Sara Kitson, Alessia Turri, Michele
Lazzaro, Christian Bazzani, Renata Balducci, Alisha Zaveri, Talia Amador,
Loida Santos, Barbara Ficarelli, Eleonora Vicari, Laura Colli Ghisalberti,
Lisa Cavallini, Tammy Corkish, Matthew Kenney, Chelsea LaSalle, the
restaurants and hotels I contacted and present in this book and all the
incredible people I have met on my travels throughout the world.

Graphics and pagination: Nicola Rossini and Roberto Rossi
Cover photo: Christian Bazzani and Roberto Rossi
Preface and english translation: Tammy Corkish
Photos: Aurelia Strassner instagram:@a.nina.nana, Christian Bazzani,
Daniela Loprevite, Giacomo Sergi instagram:giacomo_sergi_photo, Laura
Colli Ghisalberti, Tiziano Brignoli
Icone grafiche: designed by Freepik from Flaticon
September 2018

ROBERTO ROSSI was born in Arezzo in 1971. He graduated with a diploma in electronics in 1990 but always had a passion for photography and travelling thanks to his father who was a professional photographer and the many friends who inspired him to want to visit new places.

"When I was little I used to be fascinated by travel agencies. When no one was looking I would steal the glossy brochures and imagine I was in those strange and beautiful places. I was 16 when I went on my first journey to Morocco and since then I have been all over the world."

The USA always exerted a strong influence over Roberto, a nation which he has got to know gradually and intimately from the East Coast cities to the great parks and the West Coast. His first book, published in 2017, was the result of an intensely felt journey across America on Route 66 (Route 66, an American Myth is available on Amazon).

Roberto is an artist, a traveler, a motorcyclist and blogger whose blog in Italian, Vegani in Viaggio, has amassed a devoted following. His books, photos, and advice are unique and always worth taking in.

He has been a vegan for many years and a cat owner for many more.

He works manly in graphics which gives him a perfect eye for capturing an essential image. Roberto is a natural story teller and has never lost that childhood enthusiasm for discovering new places:

"Buon viaggio to everyone, whatever journeys life should offer!!"

www.veganiinviaggio.it

Screamers

Ivan Ramen

Wild ginger   Not puds

Champs diner Seitan chickeburg

Jajaja Nachos & Quesadillas

Travel Notes